DELIVER US FROM EVIL

DELIVER US FROM EVIL

What the Bible Says about Satan

MYRA B. NAGEL

United Church Press, Cleveland, Ohio

United Church Press, Cleveland, Ohio 44115

© 1999 by Myra Nagel

Printed in the United States of America on acid-free paper

04   03   02   01   00   99   5   4   3   2   1

Library of Congress Cataloging-in-Publication Data
Nagel, Myra B.
        Deliver us from evil : what the Bible says about Satan / Myra B. Nagel.
            p.   cm.
        Includes bibliographical references.
        ISBN 0-8298-1319-5 (pbk. : alk. paper)
        1. Devil—Biblical teaching.   I. Title.
    BS680.D56N34   1999
    235'47'09015—dc21

98-36234
CIP

CONTENTS

INTRODUCTION:
THE PROBLEM OF SATAN

In the months leading to the tragedy at Ruby Ridge in which an innocent woman and a young boy were killed, Randy Weaver took his family to an isolated cabin in rural Idaho to prepare for an end-time battle with the forces of evil. He expected these evil forces to be led by Jews, for according to his religious sect, Jews are the direct descendants of Satan.

In a Latin American country, priests were overwhelmed by requests for baptisms in the weeks before June 6, 1996. The date 6-6-96 came all too close to the ignominious 666, the number of "the beast," Satan's ally in Revelation 13:18. People flocked to churches for baptism against Satan's power.

As the millennium approaches, the Christian book market is flooded with titles such as *The Beginning of the End, Approaching Armageddon,* and *Escape the Coming Night,* descriptions of the battle between the armies of God and Satan during the earth's last days.[1]

To many Christians today, Satan is real, powerful, and literal. Other modern Christians relegate Satan to the same category of ideas as a flat earth and a sun that rotates around it. In many churches, Satan is mentioned rarely, almost never as a literal figure.

My three grown children, one Methodist, one Baptist, one United Church of Christ, have all, at one time or another, raised questions about Satan.

"My children's friends tell them about Satan. What shall I say to them?"

"I don't believe in a red man with horns and a forked tail, but when I look at what's going on in the world, I do think evil seems more than human."

"I know you take the Bible seriously, Mom. What exactly does the Bible say about Satan? And what do you really believe?"

I did not know how to answer their questions. I confess that as a UCC minister, I usually treated the subject of Satan as I suspect many other clergy do. I avoided it. As a parent, I did the same.

The biblical Satan is bewildering to many Christians, and I have observed that they tend to take one of two approaches to it. Either they see a literal ruler of evil as the villain of the whole Bible, or they reject the Bible's Satan language as archaic and they ignore it completely. The first approach often interprets (or misinterprets) the biblical Satan in ways that diminish personal responsibility, demonize those who hold opposing views, foster a religion of "don'ts," and focus on otherworldly goals to the neglect of problems in this world. On the other hand, Christians who ignore the Bible's Satan language miss some of the New Testament's most helpful counsel on how to deal with evil that seems larger than personal sin and how to cope with temptation that is so powerful it seems to take on a personality of its own.

I believe my children's questions are the questions of many Christians today. Evil is real in our world, and at times it truly seems more than human. Organized crime, institutional racism, the culture of poverty, and events such as the Holocaust and ethnic cleansing in Somalia and Bosnia give evidence to a force that is transpersonal, larger than individual human sin.

As my children's questions echoed in my brain, they created new questions. Can we take the Bible seriously and still ignore the figure of Satan, who clearly had a place in the thought of the

New Testament? By ignoring the passages that relate to Satan, are we throwing out the baby with the bath water? Do the biblical texts about Satan speak with any relevance to Christian life today?

In an effort to find answers, I turned to the Bible. I realize that much of our concept of Satan comes from sources outside the Bible, particularly Dante's *Inferno* and Milton's *Paradise Lost*. But I do not accept Dante or Milton as an authority for my life. If it were not for the Bible, I could easily relegate the whole idea of Satan to mythology or literature. But I cannot really ignore the Bible. Thus, the questions for me become, Given that Satan is in the Bible, and given that I take the Bible seriously, what do I really believe about Satan? How can I talk about my belief with others who hold different opinions? And most important, How does my belief affect my life? I want to know what Jesus said, what Paul said, what the book of Revelation said. Only after I have answered these questions will I be prepared to reflect thoughtfully on my belief.

If my questions are your questions, I invite you to join me in a search for answers.

As we look for references to Satan in the Bible, the first surprise may be that we find relatively few of them. In the Bible as a whole, Satan receives less emphasis than do any of the following themes: faith, faithlessness, promise, love, covenant, presence, idolatry, sin and grace, law, the poor, and justice. As we pore over the books of the Bible, concordance in hand, we will discover that Satan does not appear as a personification of evil in the entire Old Testament, and we will find only four references to Satan that are common to more than one of the Synoptic Gospels, Matthew, Mark, and Luke. In the letters of the apostle Paul, the founder of the New Testament church, we will find less mention of Satan than we might expect. By far the most significant passages about Satan occur in the Bible's last book, Revelation.

These scriptural texts will form our outline as we seek to learn what the Bible has to say about Satan. We will begin with the Hebrew word *satan* and observe its changing use in the Old Testament. We will explore some of the works that were written between the testaments, where references to Satan abound. We will search the words of Jesus and the writings of the New Testament church for their thinking on the subject, paying particular attention to the writings of Paul and to the book of Revelation.

As we seek answers, we will remember that the Bible is not one text, but a collection of texts, written over a period of fourteen hundred years. We will seek to understand each passage within its historical context before applying it to our lives today.

I invite you to set aside your preconceived notions and to journey with me through centuries of biblical thought, letting each key passage about Satan speak its own message of good and evil, faith and fear, compassion and judgment, love and hate, divine power and human responsibility. As you accompany me on this journey, I believe you will discover, as I have, that our interpretation of the Bible's references to Satan can profoundly affect the decisions we are called to make as we live day by day.

Part One

SATAN BEFORE THE TIME OF JESUS

Chapter One

SATAN IN THE OLD TESTAMENT

Hear, O Israel: The Lord our God is one Lord.
—Deuteronomy 6:4 KJV

We do not usually read a book backward. Yet that is what we are tempted to do when we study Satan in the Bible. Because the Bible's most dramatic references to Satan occur in its last book, Revelation, we are tempted to begin our study with Revelation and to interpret all the rest of scripture through its eyes. Although many popular theories of Satan have been constructed in just such a way, I believe this approach leads to a distortion of the Bible's message.

The Bible is a collection of texts written over a period of more than a thousand years. Each of its books was directed to the circumstances of its own age. Faithful biblical interpretation requires us to listen for the original meaning of each text before we examine the ways later writers have reinterpreted it. As we explore the Old Testament background of the figure of Satan, I ask you to set aside New Testament interpretations and to try to hear the words of the Old Testament as they would have been understood in their own time. When we turn to the Gospels, Paul, and Revelation, we will explore later interpretations of these earlier texts.

Satan: "Adversary" or "Accuser"

If we were able to read the Old Testament in its original Hebrew, we would discover that "satan" is the English translation of the

Hebrew word *stn*. (Hebrew words originally had no vowels.) In the first books of the Old Testament, *satan* is a common noun meaning "adversary" or "accuser." Often it is not even translated "satan," but is rendered "adversary." For example, "God's anger was kindled because he [Balaam] went: and the angel of the Lord stood in the way for an *adversary*" (Num. 22:22 KJV, emphasis added); and "David said, 'What have I to do with you, you sons of Zeruiah, that you should today become an *adversary* to me?'" (2 Sam. 19:22, emphasis added). Other times, the Hebrew *satan* is translated *"accusers"* or with words of similar meaning: "My *accusers* will be clothed with disgrace" (Ps. 109:29 NIV, emphasis added); and "Shame and ruin on *those who attack me*" (Ps. 71:13 JB, emphasis added). *Satan* in these verses is simply a common noun.

The idea that God could have any sort of evil counterpart was totally foreign to Israel's early faith. The Old Testament is, among other things, the story of a wandering tribe who clung tenaciously to their faith in one God. They held to that faith even though the events of history thrust them into the midst of one polytheistic culture after another.

Israel's story began in Ur in ancient Babylonia and moved with Abraham to Canaan. From Canaan, a famine drove Abraham's descendants to Egypt, where they eventually became slaves. Under Moses, they escaped to freedom, and after forty years in the wilderness, Joshua led them back into Canaan, the promised land, where they became a nation under judges and kings. As time went on, the tiny nation often became a pawn for its powerful neighbors, and in 597 B.C.E. it fell to the rising power of Babylonia. The Babylonians destroyed Jerusalem and took Israel's leaders into exile in Babylon, bringing them into the midst of yet another culture. Some fifty years later, when the exiles were finally allowed to return to Jerusalem, their homeland had become part of the Persian Empire.

The Canaanites, the Egyptians, the Babylonians, and the Persians all paid homage to many gods, both good and evil. Their religions were based on legends of the romances, intrigues, and battles between those gods. In contrast to the cultures that surrounded them, the Hebrew people held to the words of Deuteronomy 6:4, commonly called the *Shema*: "Hear, O Israel: The Lord is our God, the Lord alone."[1] Israel's God had no wife, no mistress, no evil opponent, no counterpart of any kind. During the first centuries of Israel's history, "satan" was nothing more than a noun that meant "adversary" or "accuser."

"The Satan"

Later in the Old Testament period, after the exiles returned from Babylon in the sixth century B.C.E., the common noun meaning "accuser" began to be applied to a person called "a satan" or "the satan." The satan was not the Ruler of Evil of the New Testament; the satan was a member of God's heavenly court who had a specific duty to perform. The satan served as a prosecuting attorney who brought charges against an accused person to aid God in the process of judgment. The satan was not God's enemy but was God's obedient servant who operated with God's permission and under God's direction.

References to "the satan" appear in three later Old Testament books.[2] The best-known references occur in Job. "There was once a man in the land of Uz whose name was Job. That man was blameless and upright, one who feared God and turned away from evil" (1:1). One day the "heavenly beings" presented themselves before God, and the satan came among them. God asked where the satan had come from, and the satan answered, "From going to and fro on the earth, and from walking up and down on it" (1:7). The satan's job as God's prosecuting attorney was to patrol the earth, searching out candidates for heavenly judgment. God asked the satan, "Have you considered my servant Job? There is no one like him on the earth, a blameless and upright man who fears God and turns away from evil" (1:8). The satan, fulfilling his assigned task as attorney for the prosecution, answered in effect, "Why shouldn't Job be a good person? You have protected him all his life. He has never known anything but ease and good fortune." Then the satan challenged God, "Stretch out your hand now, and touch all that he has, and he will curse you to your face" (1:11). God granted the satan the opportunity to test Job.

The satan, acting with God's permission, had Job's sons and daughters killed, along with his seven thousand sheep, three thousand camels, five hundred yoke of oxen, and five hundred donkeys. When Job remained faithful to God, the satan challenged God again, saying, "Stretch out your hand now and touch his bone and his flesh, and he will curse you to your face" (2:5). Again, God gave permission. At the end of the book, when Job had passed the test of faithfulness, God restored all that the satan had caused to be taken from him.

In the book of Job, the satan was God's obedient servant. He was not God's enemy, nor did he act without God's permission. He was a member of God's heavenly court, faithfully fulfilling the role as prosecuting attorney.

In the book of Zechariah, the satan again functioned as a member of the divine tribunal who brought charges against a person God was testing. Zechariah was written during the time when the exiles who had returned from captivity in Babylon were trying to rebuild the Temple. Not all Jews were enthusiastic about the project. Some of those who had not been taken into exile resented the returnees and their assumption that they could simply pick up the leadership roles they had abandoned when they were deported to Babylon.[3]

The leader of the Temple-building faction was a high priest named Joshua. One day Zechariah had a vision of Joshua appearing before the heavenly court. In the vision, the satan accused Joshua, probably voicing the objections of the faction that opposed the Temple project. Displeased with the accusation, God said, "The Lord rebuke you, O Satan! The Lord who has chosen Jerusalem rebuke you!" (3:2). The satan in Zechariah began to take on a personality, introducing a note of conflict between the satan and God.

Shortly after Zechariah was written, the writer of First Chronicles held the satan responsible for planting an evil idea in the heart of King David. "Satan stood up against Israel, and incited David to count the people of Israel" (21:1). David had ordered the census as part of his plan to impose taxation, an act that aroused strong opposition among the people.[4] The Chronicler, who clearly regarded the census as a sin, wrote, "God was displeased with this thing" (21:7). As David's punishment, God "sent a pestilence on Israel; and seventy thousand persons fell" (21:14). Thus, First Chronicles blamed the satan for David's act and its tragic consequences.

"The satan" in First Chronicles, however, is an editorial addition to a story that was first told in Second Samuel 24. In Second Samuel, the idea for the census came not from the satan, but from God! "The anger *of the Lord* was kindled against Israel, and he incited David against them, saying, 'Go, count the people of Israel and Judah'" (24:1, emphasis added). Perhaps the Chronicler saw the satan as God's agent fulfilling God's assigned task. More likely, the author added the satan to the story to avoid holding God responsible for an evil act that had disastrous consequences.

"The satan" of Job, Zechariah, and First Chronicles had begun to take on a negative personality. Still this satan was a far cry from the Satan of the New Testament, the ruler of a counter-kingdom of evil on earth. To find the Prince of Demons, Evil Ruler of this world, and God's supernatural Enemy, we must look beyond the pages of the Old Testament.

What about the Serpent, Lucifer, and the Dragon?

What about the serpent in the Garden of Eden? Revelation identified Eve's tempter as "that ancient serpent, who is the Devil and Satan" (20:2), and students of the Bible ever since have underlined this connection. If we set aside New Testament interpretations, however, we will not find any suggestion in Genesis 3 that the serpent is Satan. The serpent is not a supernatural ruler of a kingdom of evil; it is one of the earthly creatures God created. "Now the serpent was more crafty than any other wild animal *that the Lord God had made*" (Gen. 3:1, emphasis added). Walter Brueggemann, in his excellent commentary on Genesis, states that the serpent simply functions as a literary device to move the plot of the story: "It is not a phallic symbol or satan or a principle of evil or death. It is a player in the dramatic presentation."[5]

What about Lucifer, the angel who rebelled against God? Isaiah 14:12–15 noted a Day Star, "son of Dawn," who had fallen from heaven. The King James Version, following the Latin Vulgate Bible, translated "Day Star" as "Lucifer," which meant "shining one."

> How you are fallen from heaven,
> > O Day Star [Lucifer, KJV], son of Dawn!
> How you are cut down to the ground,
> > you who laid the nations low!
> You said in your heart,
> > "I will ascend to heaven;
> I will raise my throne

> above the stars of God;
> I will sit on the mount of assembly
>   on the heights of Zaphon;
> I will ascend to the tops of the clouds,
>   I will make myself like the Most High."
> But you are brought down to Sheol,
>   to the depths of the Pit.

"Lucifer," as the Latin Vulgate and the King James Version translated "Day Star," triggered the imagination of many later writers including John Milton, whose *Paradise Lost* tells an elaborate story of Lucifer's rebellion in heaven and fall to earth. The Day Star in Isaiah, however, conveyed no such meaning to its original hearers. Day Star was a metaphor Isaiah used to poke fun at Israel's archenemy, the king of Babylon. Both Day Star and Dawn were names of Canaanite gods, and the "mount of assembly on the heights of Zaphon" in verse 13 was a mountain where the gods assembled.[6] In a Canaanite myth, Attar the Day Star tried to take the place of the god Baal. When his attempt failed, Attar was forced to come down from heaven and rule on earth.[7] Isaiah's reference to the Day Star is part of a long taunting song directed to Babylon. By calling Babylon's king Day Star (Lucifer, KJV), Isaiah ridiculed him for being as pretentious as the fallen Canaanite god.

What about the sea dragon that some Old Testament texts imply God conquered and killed before the creation of the earth? Several verses in Job, the Psalms, Isaiah, Ezekiel, and Habakkuk refer to this monster, variously called Leviathan, dragon, Rahab, serpent, and sometimes simply Sea, River, or the Deep. Isaiah asked, "Was it not you [God] who cut Rahab in pieces, who pierced the dragon?" (51:9). The psalmist, calling on God's power as Creator of the world, stated, "You [God] divided the sea by your might; you broke the heads of the dragons in the waters. You crushed the heads of Leviathan" (Ps. 74:13–14). Revelation linked this dragon with the serpent of the Garden of Eden and named them both Satan: "[The angel] seized the dragon, that ancient serpent, who is the Devil and Satan" (20:2). The original hearers of Job, the Psalms, and the prophets, however, would have made no such connections. Like the Day Star, the primordial dragon referred to myths that were popular in the cultures surrounding Israel. In Canaan, the promised land where the Hebrew people settled, legends were told of a primordial dragon slain by the hero god at the time of creation. Before Canaan's most powerful god, Baal, could win out over other gods and establish authority over the earth, Baal had to kill the monsters Sea and River.

> Did I [Baal] not crush 'Il's Darling Sea?
>> Nor destroy River, the great god?
>>> Nor muzzle Tannin [the sea dragon] full well?
> I crushed the writhing serpent,
>> The accursed one of seven heads.[8]

In Babylonia, where the Hebrew people spent years in exile, they also heard myths of a primordial dragon. According to the Babylonian epic *Enuma Elis,* the hero god Marduk conquered Tiamat, goddess of chaos and the sea, then split her into two parts like a clam, formed the earth of one part, and fashioned the sky of the other part.[9]

The Old Testament sometimes refers to these creation mythologies, which were well known to its hearers. But in every case the references function to celebrate the absolute sovereignty of the God of Israel and to demonstrate the superiority of Israel's God over the false gods of surrounding cultures.

Israel's theology of the creation, narrated in Genesis, is radically different from that of the surrounding mythologies. As if to underline the superiority of the one God over the false gods of Canaanite and Babylonian mythology, Genesis 1 specifically states that God *created* the sea monster. God said, "'Let the waters bring forth swarms of living creatures, and let birds fly above the earth across the dome of the sky.' *So God created the great sea monsters* and every living creature that moves, of every kind, with which the waters swarm" (Gen. 1:20–21, emphasis added). And God looked at the earth and at all the creation, even the great sea monsters, and saw that "it was good" (Gen. 1:10, 12, 18, 21, 25).

To find an earth that is dominated by a ruler of evil, we will have to look beyond the pages of the Old Testament.

To Think About

1. When you hear someone talk about Satan, what is usually your reaction? Why?

2. Before you began reading this book, how would you have described the role of Satan in the Old Testament? What insights did you gain as you read this chapter?

3. Why is it important in Bible study to consider each book within its historical context?

4. Where do you see evil that seems larger than personal sin in our world today?

5. What have you found helpful in this chapter?

6. What have you found troubling?

Chapter Two

SATAN BETWEEN THE TESTAMENTS

The whole earth has been corrupted through the works that were taught by Azazel; to him ascribe all sin.

—1 Enoch 10:8–9

In the Old Testament, Satan is God's obedient servant. Yet in the New Testament, Satan suddenly appears as the ruler of evil, a supernatural figure who bears the responsibility for instigating all of the world's sin. When did this transformation take place? What caused this dramatic change?

We will not find the answer to these questions within the pages of our Bible. That is because the concept of a supernatural ruler of evil first appeared in Jewish literature during the period of history that falls between the end of our Old Testament and the beginning of our New Testament. Often referred to as the intertestamental period, the time that elapsed between the Old and New Testaments spans some four hundred years.

Our "Old Testament" is made up of the books contained in the Hebrew canon. "Canon" comes from a Greek word meaning "rule" or "standard." The Hebrew canon is the body of religious writings that Judaism acknowledges as divinely inspired, authoritative, and complete.

The last events of Israel's history that are explicitly recorded in the Hebrew canon took place in the fifth century before the birth of Jesus when the Jews returned from exile in Babylon and rebuilt their Temple under the leadership of Ezra and Nehemiah. Judaism believed that the prophetic period, the time when God spoke directly to the world through human prophets, came to an end with Ezra. Therefore, any literature that was dated after Ezra's time was excluded from the canon. The Hebrew canon does contain a small amount of Jewish literature that was actually written after the fifth century B.C.E., but these works were authored under pseudonyms of prophets who lived in an earlier age. The book of Daniel, for example, was almost certainly written around 165 B.C.E., but its author used the pseudonym of a prophet named Daniel, who lived during the Babylonian exile, some four centuries earlier.[1]

Judaism produced many other writings during the four centuries before the birth of Jesus. Although the works were eventually excluded from the Hebrew canon, they were familiar to the writers of the New Testament. Because the Hebrew canon was not finalized until after the earliest parts of the New Testament were written, some of the noncanonical books were still considered "scripture" at the time of Jesus.[2] Many of these writings can be found today in the Apocrypha, a group of books many Bibles include as a separate section, and in the Pseudepigrapha (pronounced soo–da–PIG–ra–fa), collections of noncanonical Jewish literature available in most large libraries.[3]

The four centuries about which our Bible is virtually silent saw history-changing events including the conquest by Alexander the Great, the spread of Greek culture throughout the biblical lands, and the eventual domination by the Roman Empire. If we wish to witness the transformation of Satan from God's servant to God's supernatural enemy, we must turn to the Jewish literature that was written during the period between the testaments.

A Supernatural Ruler of Evil

A supernatural ruler of evil makes a grand entrance in some of the intertestamental literature. One such work is the Book of

Watchers, which later became chapters 1–36 of First Enoch, one of the books of the Pseudepigrapha. The Book of Watchers, like many other works of its time, was written under the pseudonym of an ancient figure. Its author introduces himself as Enoch, a seventh generation descendant of Adam and Eve and the father of Methuselah. Enoch was briefly mentioned in Genesis as a man who "walked with God" (5:18–24).

In the Book of Watchers, Enoch learns in a vision that evil first came into the world when watcher angels, appointed by God to oversee earthly activities, betrayed their divine responsibility by taking human wives. "And it came to pass when the children of men had multiplied that in those days were born unto them beautiful and comely daughters. And the angels, the children of the heaven, saw and lusted after them, and said to one another: 'Come, let us choose us wives from among the children of men and beget us children'" (1 Enoch 6:1–3).[4]

Thus, the stage is set for an evil leader of the watcher angels. The Old Testament contained glimpses of rebellious angels, but they had no leader. In the Book of Watchers, however, the rebellion of the watcher angels is instigated by an evil commander, variously called Semjaza, Azazel, and in the later part of First Enoch, Satan. The different names occur because several different stories about Enoch were written during the intertestamental period, and these stories give different names to the demonic leader. Eventually, these works were combined to make up the final text of First Enoch. Whether named Semjaza, Azazel, or Satan, the supernatural ruler of evil in First Enoch mobilizes the spirits of the watcher angels so that they continue to "afflict, oppress, destroy, attack, do battle, and work destruction on the earth" (1 Enoch 15:8–12). Enoch assures his readers, however, that the evil worked by the watcher angels will soon end! In another vision, Enoch learns that God, not Satan, controls human destiny. A cosmic battle will herald the final consummation of history. Then the evil angels will be bound hand and foot and thrown into a pit to await final judgment (1 Enoch 10:6–7; 19:1). When the day of judgment comes, Azazel (Satan) will be "cast into the fire" (1 Enoch 10:7). But the "righteous and holy" will sit at the feet of the throne of God and eat the fruit of a fragrant tree whose "leaves and blooms wither not forever" (1 Enoch 24:3–25:5).

A New Type of Literature

The Book of Watchers is an example of a new type of literature that came into flower during the intertestamental period. This new strain of thought was called apocalyptic, from the Hebrew word *apocalypse,* meaning "to reveal" or "to uncover."[5] Apocalyptic literature contained revelations about a cosmic conflict taking place between supernatural forces of good and evil and about God's eventual triumph in this battle. These revelations took the form of fantastic imagery and bizarre symbolism that only those within the circle of faith could interpret.

Apocalypticism attempted to answer the question, How can a good and all-powerful God allow the existence of evil in the world? In many respects, apocalypticism was a continuation of Old Testament prophecy. Prophets such as Amos, Isaiah, and Jeremiah were also concerned with the world's evil. They saw God at work in history, moving events toward the conquering of evil and the eventual coming of God's reign. But the Old Testament prophets saw evil as human, not supernatural, in origin. When the nation suffered a disaster, such as the destruction of Jerusalem and the Temple by the Babylonians in 597 B.C.E., the prophets interpreted these events as God's judgment upon the people of Israel for their sin. The Old Testament prophets expected God's victory over evil to take place on this earth. They did not expect the coming of God's reign to bring an end to human history.

In contrast, apocalyptic writers saw evil as more than human. Earthly struggles were part of a larger battle between good and evil that was taking place in the heavens. They believed that all human history was part of this battle and that God was leading this world toward a climactic end. The apocalyptic visions revealed that the earth's last days were rapidly approaching. In fact, the current suffering should be interpreted as a sign that God would soon inaugurate a new age in a world beyond this one.

Apocalyptic literature such as the Book of Watchers (First Enoch) was popular during the intertestamental period. The rebellious watcher angels also appear in Jubilees, another book of the Pseudepigrapha, which was written somewhat later than the Book of Watchers.[6] In Jubilees, which claimed to be authored by Moses, the leader of the watcher angels is named Mastema, from the Hebrew word for "enmity."

In other apocalyptic literature of the period, a supernatural ruler of evil is named Belial (Worthless One) and Samael (Angel of Poison).[7] Satan appears in many of the Qumran Documents, better known as the Dead Sea Scrolls. The War Rule, for example, is a description of an end-time battle that pits the "sons of light, [the true Israel], against the company of the sons of darkness, the army of Satan."[8]

Where did apocalypticism come from? Why did this new type of prophecy that spawned a demonic ruler of evil suddenly appear in Jewish literature? What caused Judaism to begin to conceive of evil as supernatural in origin at this particular point in its history?

One answer to these questions is that apocalyptic ideas came to Israel from the religions of surrounding nations, particularly Persia, which ruled the Hebrew nation before the rise of Alexander the Great and, even after that, continued to influence the culture of the entire region. Zoroastrianism of Persia saw the entire history of the cosmos as a struggle between the forces of good, aligned with the god Ahura Mazda, and the forces of evil, led by the sinister Angra Mainyu.[9] Many scholars believe that Persian dualism, the cosmic struggle between good and evil, was one of the roots of Jewish apocalyptic thought. But the influence of Persian ideas is not the whole answer.

Crisis Literature

A more important explanation for the rise of Jewish apocalyptic literature is that these stories of cosmic battles between good and evil were written to reassure Jews at a time when their faith and traditions were deeply threatened. During the intertestamental period, orthodox Jews feared for the survival of their faith in the face of the onslaught of Greek civilization. In 333 B.C.E., Greek armies led by Alexander the Great had conquered the region of Judea, making it a part of the Greek Empire. Conflict between orthodox Judaism and Greek culture pervaded the whole intertestamental period.

At times this conflict was open and obvious. In the second century before the birth of Jesus, the Greek ruler Antiochus Epiphanes decided to rid his territory of Judaism.[10] He ordered all copies of the Torah burned. He erected an altar to the Greek god Zeus in the Temple. And he threatened death to anyone who refused to bow down to the Greek god.

The Old Testament book of Daniel, the only complete apocalyptic book in the Bible, was written during this period of persecution. In symbolic imagery, Daniel portrayed the Greek Empire as a dragonlike creature that had a small horn with "eyes like human eyes." In a clear reference to Antiochus, this beast had "a mouth speaking arrogantly" (Dan. 7:1–8). Through its fantastic imagery, the book of Daniel assured its readers in 165

B.C.E. that the persecution under Antiochus would soon end. Daniel learned in a vision that the heavenly court had already met and judged the Greek Empire (the dragonlike beast) and its ruler Antiochus Epiphanes (the mouth speaking arrogantly). Very soon, God would lead the forces of good in a cosmic battle, and the faithful would be delivered. Thus, the apocalyptic book of Daniel offered hope to Jews in a time of crisis.

A Graver Crisis

The persecution under Antiochus, although blatant and obvious, was not the most serious threat to Judaism posed by Greek domination during the centuries between the testaments. This period of *persecution* was, in fact, quite brief. A graver threat to orthodox Judaism arose not from persecution by Greek rulers, but instead from their conquerors' *invitation to join their culture!* Although the threat was more subtle, it was much more alarming from the perspective of devout Jews.

Alexander the Great and his successors had introduced new ideas and a different lifestyle to the backward region of Judea. Many Jews were drawn to the attractive Greek culture, known as Hellenism.[11] Greek art, sculpture, literature, and drama dazzled the Jews, whose own culture had produced nothing comparable. Many Jews, particularly among the wealthier and more sophisticated classes, wanted to attend Greek theater and to compete in public athletic competitions in the *gymnasion.* They wanted their sons to have all the benefits offered by a Greek education. And they wanted to participate in Greek commerce. All the advantages of the Greek culture were open to Jews who were willing to set aside their Jewish traditions and adopt Greek ways.

To the more traditional Jews, however, Hellenism was deeply threatening. Greek science and mathematics introduced unsettling new ways of looking at the world. Even more alarming,

Greek philosophers disdained the authority of a divinely inspired scripture, believing that access to the divine will could be gained through reason. The author of Second Maccabees, one of the books in the Apocrypha, warned that Hellenism was causing Jews to forsake their laws and traditions: "There was such an extreme of Hellenization and increase in the adoption of foreign ways . . . that the priests were no longer intent upon their service at the altar. Despising the sanctuary and neglecting the sacrifices, they hurried to take part in the unlawful proceedings in the wrestling arena after the signal for the discus-throwing, disdaining the honors prized by their ancestors and putting the highest value upon Greek forms of prestige" (2 Macc. 4:13–15).

In the eyes of the most traditional and strict Jews, the fight against the tidal wave of Greek ideas and institutions was the deepest crisis Judaism had ever faced. Believing that God's favor depended on the strict observance of their laws and rituals, orthodox Jews watched helplessly as Hellenism insinuated itself into the internal fabric of their religious community, corrupting every office in Judaism including even the high priest (2 Macc. 4:7–10). The struggle against Hellenism was a battle for Israel's soul! Could faith in the God of their ancestors survive this cancer growing from within?

Apocalyptic works such as First Enoch and Jubilees answered with a resounding *yes!* They assured devout Jews that God had not sanctioned the evil forces they saw at work in their society; evil was caused by rebellious angels who had betrayed their divine responsibility. God was fighting evil. And God's victory would come soon. Although the earth had fallen under the sway of Satan, God controlled human destiny. The present tribulation was a sign that God's day of judgment was near. In God's new age, evil would be punished and faithfulness rewarded. God's justice would reign.

The Intimate Enemy

We may observe that it was the struggle *within* Judaism that seemed to give rise to the concept of a supernatural ruler of evil. Satan does not appear in the Old Testament book of Daniel, which addresses the struggle of a united Israel against a common enemy. In Daniel, Israel's enemies are represented as great beasts—terrible, but not supernatural.[12] On the other hand, the intertestamental writings that feature a supernatural ruler of evil seem to address the divisions within Judaism, the struggle between the orthodox and the Hellenizing Jews.

Elaine Pagels, in *The Origin of Satan,* suggests that the watcher angels, led by the rebellious angel Semjaza/Azazel/Mastema/Satan, represented particular members of their authors' society. The rebellious angels may have been a contemptuous reference to Greek rulers who, like the watcher angels, claimed to descend from the gods and demanded to be worshiped as divine. Or, Pagels suggests, the watcher angels may have been a satiric reference to members of the Jerusalem priesthood who violated their divinely given responsibility by aligning themselves with the pagan Greek culture.[13]

Pagels also argues persuasively that Satan emerged as the "intimate enemy," the betraying brother or sister within the family of Judaism. She states, "Whatever version of [Satan's] origin one chooses, then, and there are many, all depict Satan as an *intimate* enemy—the attribute that qualifies him so well to express conflict among Jewish groups. Those who asked, 'How could God's own angel become his enemy?' were thus asking, in effect, 'How could one of *us* become one of *them?*'"[14]

Whatever the reasons may have been, Judaism in the late first century ultimately rejected apocalyptic works that featured an otherworldly ruler of evil for inclusion into the Hebrew canon. Then as now, Judaism has leaned away from a belief in a supernatural origin of evil.

Nevertheless, apocalypticism, which held the rebellious angel Satan responsible for the world's evil and expected God to triumph over this enemy in cosmic combat at the consummation of human history, was a commonly known and widely accepted strain of thought at the beginning of the New Testament period.

To Think About

1. How did living in the midst of Greek culture pose a threat to the faith of traditional Jews?

2. Is there a struggle between faith and culture today? What are some examples? How do you experience this struggle personally?

3. How would you define "evil"?

4. Apocalypticism attempted to answer the question, How can a good and all-powerful God allow the existence of evil? How would *you* answer this question?

5. What did you find helpful in this chapter?

6. What did you find troubling?

Part Two

SATAN IN THE GOSPELS

Chapter Three

SATAN AND PERSONAL RESPONSIBILITY

[Jesus] was in the wilderness forty days, tempted by Satan.
—Mark 1:13

Recently, a judge pronounced a life sentence on a man convicted of manslaughter for killing three teenagers while he was driving under the influence of alcohol and drugs. His attorney, protesting the severity of the sentence, declared, "The Devil is to blame for this tragedy!"

Doubtless the attorney sincerely believed that he was accurately representing the teaching of the New Testament. Certainly, his view of Satan is common in our society. But I think similar comments distort the teaching of Jesus on the subject of evil. They confuse Christians who are trying to take the Bible seriously. And in so doing, they discredit Christianity as a whole.

My disagreement with the defense attorney does not center on the question of whether Satan is real. Too much debate among modern Christians has focused on questions such as, Do you believe in Satan? or Do you take the idea of Satan literally? The issue of whether Satan is real is not the central question for Christians to debate. The central question is, What does the Bible teach us about the power of evil and our response to it? Whether or not one takes Satan literally, the defense attorney who tried to lessen his client's guilt by blaming the Devil distorted the Bible's teaching about personal responsibility in the face of temptation.

We have seen that the New Testament was written in a time when a belief in a supernatural ruler of evil was widely accepted. Thus, it makes many references to Satan or the Devil. ("Devil," *diabolos,* is the Greek translation of the Hebrew word *satan.*) But the New Testament's Satan language was not addressed to the question of literal belief; it sought answers to questions of everyday life. How are persons of faith to respond to evil that seems overwhelming or to temptation so strong that it seems to take on a personality of its own? Is God faithful? Is God powerful? What does God want us to do? Will God help us? These are the questions to which the New Testament's Satan language is addressed. These are the questions we must answer if we are to understand the Bible's use of "Satan" and to interpret its meaning for our own lives.

As we explore the New Testament's references to Satan, I suggest that we set aside temporarily the issue of literal belief and try to listen to the Scripture's teaching about the power of evil as it affects our lives. We will turn first to the Gospels and then to the New Testament church, focusing on the letters of Paul and the book of Revelation.

Satan and Jesus

What did Jesus say about Satan? Although we cannot be sure of his precise words, we have the testimony of the Gospels, which were compiled from stories about Jesus that had been told and retold. Matthew, Mark, and Luke are often called the Synoptic Gospels because they are similar in structure and they share large amounts of identical material. Most biblical research indicates that Mark, dated around 65–70, was the first Gospel to be written and that Matthew and Luke used Mark as one of their sources. John is dated somewhat later, and most scholars agree that it contains more editorial additions to the earliest sources than do the Synoptics. We cannot look behind the written Gospels to determine with certainty the exact words of Jesus, but I believe that if we focus on the references to Satan that are common to at least two of the Synoptic Gospels, we will gain a representative view of Jesus' teaching about the power of evil in our lives.[1]

Only four references to Satan are common to more than one of the Synoptic Gospels. The first is the story of Jesus' temptation in the wilderness (Matt. 4:1–11; Mark 1:12–13; Luke 4:1–13). A second occurs when the Pharisees accuse Jesus of casting out demons by the power of Beelzebul, and Jesus responds, "Would Satan cast out Satan?" (Matt. 12:22–37; Mark 3:22–30; Luke 11:14–23). In a third incident, Peter protests when Jesus tells the disciples that he must suffer and die, and Jesus responds to Peter, "Get behind me, Satan!" (Matt. 16:21–23; Mark 8:31–33). Jesus' parable of the sower contains a fourth reference to Satan when Jesus explains that the seed represents God's Word and Satan takes away the seed (Matt. 13:18–23; Mark 4:13–20; Luke 8:11–15). Each of these stories offers us insight into the Gospels' teaching about the power of evil and the way we are to respond to it.

In this chapter, we will look at the story of Jesus' temptation in the wilderness. The following three chapters will explore the other three references to Satan that are common to more than one Synoptic Gospel.

Temptation in the Wilderness

The first mention of Satan in Matthew, Mark, and Luke appears in the story of Jesus' temptation in the wilderness. In Mark, the story is brief: "And the Spirit immediately drove him out into the wilderness. He was in the wilderness forty days, tempted by Satan; and he was with the wild beasts; and the angels waited on him" (Mark 1:12–13). Matthew and Luke, apparently working from an independent source, both tell a more elaborate story of Jesus' personal struggle with three specific temptations, temptations we will explore in the following pages.

We may note that this incident had no witnesses, and no one suggests that Jesus himself wrote an account of it. Thus, the historical details that underlie this story are uncertain. Yet it appears in the same position in all three Synoptic Gospels. The Gospel writers obviously believed it had something important to say about temptation as it confronted Jesus and as it would also confront his followers.

In all three of the Synoptic Gospels, Jesus' temptation immediately follows his baptism by John the Baptist. Baptism was obviously a powerful experience for Jesus. He felt and saw "the Spirit descending like a dove" and heard a voice from heaven saying, "You are my Son, the Beloved" (Mark 1:9–11). Baptism seems to be the moment when Jesus felt the call to claim his role as God's Anointed One and to proclaim God's message to the world. Yet Jesus did not begin his public ministry immediately. Instead, the Spirit "drove him out into the wilderness" where he remained forty days, "tempted by Satan" (Mark 1:12–13).

The wilderness, although it may be a specific place, is certainly also a metaphor for an internal testing ground. It is related to the wilderness of Exodus and Deuteronomy where God tested the people of Israel after they escaped from bondage in Egypt and before they entered the promised land. Jesus' forty days of testing correspond to Israel's forty years in the wilderness, a place of wandering and struggle.

Did Jesus struggle with the temptation to ignore God's call? Surely, he knew that the decision to proclaim God's message to the world would have profound consequences for his personal life. He would give up many of the joys and comforts he might otherwise have expected—safety, security, the warmth of a home, and the love of a wife and family with whom he might grow old. The path to which God called him would require placing God's will above his own desires. It would bring hardship, discomfort, danger, exhaustion, pain, and early death. Could he face all that? Did he want to? Jesus was fully human as well as divine. Was he tempted to choose another road?

Jesus' Answers to Temptation

Satan's first temptation was directed to Jesus' physical comfort. Having fasted for forty days and nights, Jesus was famished. Satan said, "If you are the Son of God, command this stone to become a loaf of bread" (Luke 4:3). "Bread" here represents not only food but all basic human needs—shelter, clothing, sexual fulfillment. In modern terms, it is the temptation to want more than we need, to squander our energy accumulating fine food and drink, stylish clothes, luxurious homes, or sexual conquests, to let our perceived "needs" replace God's will as top priority in our lives. For Jesus, it was the temptation to place his hunger for food ahead of his hunger for God's Spirit.

Jesus answered the Tempter by quoting from Deuteronomy's account of Moses' farewell speech to the Israelites at the end of their forty years in the wilderness: "It is written, 'One does not live by bread alone'" (Luke 4:4; Deut. 8:3).

In the second temptation, as Luke tells the story, the Devil led Jesus up to a high place and showed him all the kingdoms of the world. He said to Jesus, "To you I will give their glory and all this authority; for it has been given over to me, and I give it to anyone I please. If you, then, will worship me, it will all be yours" (Luke 4:6–7).

Coming from the tiny, unimportant village of Nazareth, Jesus had no wealth, social status, or religious position. In the world's eyes, he was a nobody. Satan offered him the power to rise from

the bottom of society to the top. Everything the world values—
money, power, status—could be his. In fact, if he said yes to
Satan, Jesus could rule the whole world.

The temptation to worship the world's values is all too familiar to us. In his book *A Call to Conversion* Jim Wallis states our
problem succinctly: "That which commands our time, energy,
and thoughts is what we really worship."[2] Where do we spend
more of our time, energy, and thought? On God's priorities and
will for our lives? Or on possessions, money, prestige, power, and
status? How much of our nation's foreign policy is motivated by
our desire to preserve our economic interests, our energy supply,
and our affluent way of life? How can we say no to these overwhelming temptations?

Jesus found the power to turn from the world's values, as he
had found strength to resist the temptation to turn stones into
bread, by remembering the laws God gave God's people through
Moses. Quoting again from Deuteronomy, he said, "It is written, 'Worship the Lord your God, and serve only him'" (Luke
4:8; Deut. 6:13).

In the third and last temptation, according to Luke, the Devil
took Jesus to Jerusalem and placed him on the pinnacle of the
Temple. There the Devil challenged him, quoting from the
Psalms, "If you are the Son of God, throw yourself down from
here, for it is written, 'He will command his angels concerning
you, to protect you,' and 'On their hands they will bear you up,
so that you will not dash your foot against a stone'" (Luke
4:9–11; Ps. 91:11–12). This is the temptation to test God by setting up requirements for what God must do. It is like saying,
"Prove that you are God by saving me from my own reckless-
ness," or "Prove that you are God by helping me get a promo-
tion or first place in the art show," or "Prove that you are God
by healing my child."

During their wanderings in the wilderness, the Israelites tested God in just such a way at a place called Massah, named from the Hebrew verb for "test." The Israelites demanded, "Give us water to drink," asking, "Is the Lord among us or not?" (Exod. 17:2–7).

Jesus remembered Massah when Satan tempted him to throw himself from a pinnacle to prove that God could save him. Quoting Moses' words in Deuteronomy 6:16, Jesus answered Satan, "Do not put the Lord your God to the test" (Luke 4:12). The full text from Deuteronomy is "Do not put the Lord your God to the test, as you tested him at Massah."

After Jesus had answered all three temptations, Satan departed. Then, according to Matthew, "angels came and waited on him" (4:11). Immediately after that experience, Jesus returned to Galilee filled with the power of the Spirit, and he embarked on his public ministry.

Jesus' actions from that point on demonstrate that his struggle with temptation was behind him. Secure in the faith that "one does not live by bread alone," he moved from village to village proclaiming God's message and trusting God to provide the next meal. And when he sent his disciples out to preach the gospel, he instructed them, "Take nothing for your journey, no staff, nor bag, nor bread, nor money—not even an extra tunic" (Luke 9:3).

Resisting all temptation to worship worldly values, Jesus spent time with those whom society considered second-class citizens and even outcasts. He praised the lowly and attacked the powerful for hypocrisy, greed, and lack of compassion. He rejected political power and the temptation to rule by force, and he opted instead to change the world by transforming individual hearts.

He had no need to test God. He faced hardship, discomfort, danger, exhaustion, suffering, and even death with an inner peace that can come only from deep faith. And when the shadow of the cross drew near, he prayed simply, "Not what I want, but what you want" (Mark 14:36).

Temptation and Faith

What does the story of Jesus and Satan in the wilderness say to us about the power of temptation in our lives?

First, evil is real. Temptation is part of life. If Jesus faced such powerful temptation, who among us can be immune? At times, temptation may be so powerful that it seems almost impossible to resist, so powerful that it seems to take on a personality of its own.

Second, evil is deceptive. Evil can masquerade as good. At first glance, all of Satan's temptations might look harmless. What was wrong with bread? Did not Jesus teach his disciples to pray, "Give us this day our daily bread"? Yes, but Jesus saw that Satan was tempting him to try to satisfy spiritual hunger with physical food. What was wrong with gaining power to rule the earth? Was not Jesus' ultimate mission to bring God's reign to the world? Yes, but Satan was not promoting God's reign. Satan offered worldly power and worldly glory. What was wrong with taking a risk and trusting in God's help? Is that not what faith means? Yes, but true faith does not set up tests for God or demand a specific miracle in order to prove that God is God. The story of Jesus and Satan warns us that evil can look a lot like good. And we know it is true. We may tell ourselves, "This lie is necessary," or "This extramarital affair is bringing me personal growth," or "This small deception in my business practice will make it possible for me to give more to charity." Evil is deceptive, and the tendency to rationalize is very human.

Third, struggle is essential to a life of faith. As the Spirit drove Jesus into the wilderness, the Spirit calls us to enter the wilderness that lies within ourselves and to deal honestly with what we find there. Because evil is attractive and deceptive, it can catch

us unaware. We may drift into it, pretending all is well, ratio-
nalizing our actions, barely realizing that we have made a con-
scious choice. The example of Jesus asks us to face temptation
squarely, to look at the likely consequences of our actions, to
struggle with our choices, and to seek to follow God's will.

Fourth, persons of faith have the power to resist temptation. No
supernatural force renders us helpless. We may tend to think
that Jesus' power to resist temptation was mystic and mysterious,
something unique to Jesus. Jesus was, of course, unique. But to
interpret this story as a lesson about Jesus' unique power to resist
Satan would miss the point. The resources that gave Jesus the
strength to resist temptation are also available to us. Faced with
temptation, Jesus filled his mind with scripture, which he knew
by heart. He recalled the words Moses spoke to the Israelites at
the end of their wilderness journey. He remembered God's law
and God's blessing. We can assume that he also asked for God's
guidance and help. In short, he drew on the strength that grew
from a lifetime of studying God's Word, obeying God's law, and
trusting that same Spirit who drove him into the wilderness.
God's power comes to us through the same channels. In our
toughest decisions, we can call on the strength we gain from
habits of faithfulness, habits that are formed day by day, hour
by hour, and decision by decision.

Finally, the power to resist temptation belongs to us. We are
responsible for our actions. The attorney who tried to hold the
Devil responsible for his client's manslaughter would find no
support in this story. Although evil is real and deceptive, those
who live in faith and faithfulness have the power to resist. "The
Devil made me do it" is not an adequate excuse. The example of
Jesus calls us to enter the wilderness of honest struggle. It urges
us to rely on the resources of our faith, where we will find the
strength to resist temptation. It asks us to remember and obey

God's will in our decisions both large and small. And it promises that the Spirit who calls us into the wilderness will not abandon us there.

To Think About

1. When in your life have you experienced a "wilderness," that is, a period of wandering, struggle, or testing? Looking back with hindsight, how was the "wilderness" a positive and/or negative experience?

2. When have you experienced temptation so large that it seemed to take on a personality of its own?

3. What is the greatest temptation in your life right now? How is God calling you to struggle with this temptation?

4. Do you agree with this statement: "The resources that gave Jesus the strength to resist temptation are also available to us"? What helped Jesus deal with temptation? What helps you?

5. What do you see as the relationship between sin, its consequences, responsibility, and forgiveness or grace?

Chapter Four

SATAN AND COMPASSION

How can Satan cast out Satan?

—Mark 3:23

If we were to present evidence in a court of law to demonstrate what Jesus said about Satan, we would have to classify the story of Jesus' temptation in the wilderness as hearsay. No witnesses were present, and none of the Gospel writers suggest that Jesus himself wrote an account. The next reference to Satan that is common to the Synoptic Gospels, however, contains sayings that even the most skeptical biblical scholars attribute to the historical Jesus.[1]

The story begins with a miraculous healing. Jesus healed a man who was unable to speak (Matt. 12:22–37; Mark 3:20–30; Luke 11:14–23).[2] While many observers marveled, some scribes and Pharisees were offended.[3] They said, "He casts out demons by Beelzebul, the ruler of the demons" (Luke 11:15). Originally a Canaanite god, Beelzebul eventually had become another name for Satan.[4]

According to all three Synoptic Gospels, Jesus answered the charge in words similar to these: "Every kingdom divided against itself is laid waste, and no city or house divided against itself will stand. If Satan casts out Satan, he is divided against himself; how then will his kingdom stand?" (Matt. 12:25–26). Jesus was angry. Were his accusers suggesting that Satan would cast out demons? Then Satan would be working against Satan, splitting up Satan's own house or city or kingdom! Ridiculous! Impossible!

Although Mark's setting for this encounter is different, the central core of his story agrees with Matthew and Luke. Mark sets the charge against Jesus within a story about Jesus' family. When his family heard about Jesus' preaching and healing, they went out to restrain him because people were saying, "He has gone out of his mind" (3:21). The rumor, literally translated "he is beside himself," implied that Jesus was possessed by a demon. Mark makes this implication explicit in verse 30: "They [the gossipers] had said, 'He has an unclean spirit.'" Jesus responded to the accusation, as in Matthew and Luke, "How can Satan cast out Satan? . . . If Satan has risen up against himself and is divided, he cannot stand, but his end has come" (3:23, 26).

Blasphemy against the Spirit

Mark then takes Jesus' indignation a step farther, adding, "Truly I tell you, people will be forgiven for their sins and whatever blasphemies they utter; but whoever blasphemes against the Holy Spirit can never have forgiveness, but is guilty of an eternal sin" (3:28–29). To attribute Jesus' work of healing and "casting out demons" to Satan is the worst sin one can commit!

This story addresses the question of what people of faith are to do when confronted with persons or ideas we believe are evil. While we may not want to identify with the Pharisees or scribes who accused Jesus, that is what the story asks us to consider.

The Pharisees and scribes were persons of deep faith. They were the religious leaders of their day, well trained, and thoroughly grounded in the Scripture. They were deeply concerned with issues of right and wrong. They were conscientious and devout. They devoted their whole lives to interpreting God's law and to obeying it.

These are admirable traits. Yet while we may identify with these qualities, the story pushes us to ask some questions. How certain are we of our own righteousness? How confident are we of our capacity to discern God's will in every place and circumstance? Do we have the ability—and the authority—to judge that another person is an instrument of Satan?

The Pharisees, secure in their own righteousness, felt qualified to discern good from evil. They did not hesitate to judge others. And they were convinced that the untrained, itinerant preacher named Jesus, who held no place in the religious hierarchy and whose ideas often sharply contradicted their own, could not possibly be an instrument for God's work in the world. So certain were they of their judgment that they accused Jesus not only of being wrong, but also of operating with the power of Satan.

Over the centuries, Christians have suggested that Satan's "armies" include, among others, Copernicus, Galileo, Charles Darwin, Sigmund Freud, John Dewey, and Dr. Benjamin Spock; Germans, Russians, and Iranians; Muslims, Jews, and Protestants; astronomers, liberals, and biblical scholars who attempt to discern when and by whom various parts of the Bible were written. All these accusations have been made by people who, like the Pharisees, sincerely believed they were right. Yet does any human being have the authority to label another person as "possessed by Satan"? Can any of us be certain that we know all of God's truth? Even using the Scripture as our authority, can we be sure that we know the only correct interpretation of every verse? Could we be mistaken, as the Pharisees were?

Jesus' Warnings against Judging Others

Throughout his ministry, Jesus warned about the dangers of judging others. "Do not judge, so that you may not be judged," he said (Matt. 7:1; Luke 6:37). For people who were confident of their own moral superiority, Jesus told a parable about a Pharisee and a tax collector who went to the Temple to pray. The Pharisee prayed boldly, "God, I thank you that I am not like other people: thieves, rogues, adulterers, or even like this tax collector." The Pharisee, and most other Jews as well, regarded the tax collector as an obvious sinner, a man who had sold his soul to work for the oppressive Roman government and who regularly cheated his Jewish brothers and sisters. Perhaps the tax collector viewed himself in the same way. With eyes downcast, he beat his breast and prayed, "God, be merciful to me, a sinner!" But Jesus condemned the Pharisee and praised the humble tax collector, saying, "I tell you, this man went down to his home justified rather than the other; for all who exalt themselves will be humbled, but all who humble themselves will be exalted" (Luke 18:9–14).

Jesus' parable of the weeds or tares is directed to followers who were concerned about defining what is good against the backdrop of the world's evil. After the wheat was sown, an "enemy," probably a reference to Satan, sowed weeds in the same field while everyone slept. When the householder's servants asked the householder whether they should pull out the weeds, the householder's response, according to Jesus, was this: "No; for in gathering the weeds you would uproot the wheat along with them. Let both of them grow together until the harvest; and at harvest time I will tell the reapers, 'Collect the weeds first and bind them in bundles to be burned, but gather the wheat into my barn'" (Matt. 13:24–30). Ultimate judgment is God's province.

Human beings have the ability and the responsibility to make judgments about how to speak and act, about what to teach children, and about what position the church should take on issues in society. We have the ability and the responsibility to speak out against words and actions that offend our values, to fight against evil as we understand it, and to pass and enforce just laws. But when we label another person as an agent of Satan, we have moved beyond human authority into the realm of ultimate judgment. That realm belongs to God. Jesus called the Pharisees' accusation that he had healed by the power of Satan a blasphemy against the Holy Spirit. For us, labeling another person as an instrument of Satan risks committing such blasphemy. Like the Pharisees, we could be wrong.

The Demand for a Sign

Luke adds a valuable insight to the core of the story that is common to all three Synoptics. In Luke, not only did some of the witnesses to Jesus' healing accuse him of operating by the power of the Ruler of Demons, but others "tested" Jesus by demanding a sign from heaven: "Now [Jesus] was casting out a demon that was mute; when the demon had gone out, the one who had been mute spoke, and the crowds were amazed. But some of them said, 'He casts out demons by Beelzebul, the ruler of the demons.' *Others, to test him, kept demanding from him a sign from heaven*" (Luke 11:14–16, emphasis added). After Jesus answered the charge of demon possession, he addressed the request for a sign. He said, "If it is by the finger of God that I cast out the demons, then the kingdom of God has come to you" (v. 20). He was saying, in effect, "You saw a sign of the reign of God when I healed the man who could not speak, and you didn't even recognize it!"

In chapter 7, Luke had already addressed the issue of signs that identified Jesus as the Messiah. John the Baptist had sent word from prison, asking, "Are you the one who is to come?" Jesus, who had just cured many people of disease and blindness, responded, "Go and tell John what you have seen and heard: the blind receive their sight, the lame walk, the lepers are cleansed, the deaf hear, the dead are raised, the poor have good news brought to them" (vv. 18–22). Jesus' acts of healing were not signs of demonic power. To anyone who had eyes to see, they were signs of the reign of God!

Why might Luke have added to the story witnesses who failed to recognize Jesus' healing power as a sign of God's reign? I believe he wanted to emphasize the point that spiritual pride can blind us to God's purposes. The Pharisees' self-righteousness blinded them to the plight of the person who could not speak. Judgmentalism robbed them of compassion. It blinded them to the obvious evidence that God was at work in Jesus' act of healing. When we label another person or idea as "of Satan," we lose our ability to view that person or to investigate that idea with anything that approaches an open mind. The label itself closes off all discussion, all listening, all objective investigation. It prevents us from asking some important questions. Is this person producing good or harm? How does this person's experience differ from my own? How does that experience affect his or her decisions and actions? What are the underlying causes of this person's negative behavior? Poverty? Drugs? Discrimination? What can I do that is helpful in this situation?

Luke's addition of the witnesses who were blind to the sign of God's reign that was taking place before their eyes invites us to assess the acuity of our vision. How might our tendency to "demonize" our enemies produce spiritual obliviousness? How might it rob us of compassion? What signs of the reign of God at work in our midst might our tendency to judge others prevent us from seeing?

Gathering versus Scattering

Still another element of the story, found in Matthew and Luke, concerns gathering versus scattering. Jesus said, "Whoever is not with me is against me, and whoever does not gather with me scatters" (Matt. 12:30; Luke 11:23). The followers of Jesus are to gather, to unite, to reconcile, and to bring together; they are not to scatter or divide. To label another person or an opposing camp as an agent of Satan eradicates listening, ends communication, destroys objectivity, and erases any vestige of goodwill. It divides and scatters. It is the opposite of gathering, joining together, and building community.

What Are We to Do?

How, then, are we to react to persons and ideas we sincerely believe are contrary to God's purpose? If we are not to label persons and ideas that we consider evil as instruments of Satan, what are we to do? Do we say that everything is okay? Shall we just be nice and swallow our indignation? No! We are called to proclaim God's Word as we understand it and to resist evil as we understand it. We are called to make prayerful judgments about our own actions. In our families, we are called to set rules, guidelines, and value structures. In the church, the community, and the larger society, we are called to proclaim what we believe and why we believe it. We are called to name the wrongs we see and to work to correct them. We can do all this without labeling any person as an instrument of Satan.

We can lead by our example. We can speak, vote, organize, demonstrate, and boycott. At the same time, we can ask questions and listen to the answers. We can claim our opinions by saying, "I believe . . . ," "I feel strongly that . . . ," or "I disagree." We can seek to understand the experience of others and to learn how that experience has led to feelings and actions that are different from our own. We can remain open to the possibility that at times, like the Pharisees, we might be wrong. No matter how deeply we disagree with another person or group, we can remind ourselves that our opponents are human beings who are loved by

God even when their actions cause God pain. And we can follow the counsel of Jesus: "Love your enemies, do good to those who hate you, bless those who curse you, pray for those who abuse you" (Luke 6:27–28; Matt. 5:44).

To Think About

1. With whom do you most identify in this story? The person who begged for healing? A Pharisee? Jesus? Why?

2. Retell the story from the perspective of each of these characters. How does the story change as you see it from different perspectives?

3. When have your cries for help (even silent cries) been ignored? How did you feel? What cries for help are being ignored in your community and in the larger society?

4. When have you substituted judgment for compassion?

5. How might the tendency to "demonize" others produce "blindness"? Can you think of some examples?

6. Do you think that any human being has the authority to label another person as an agent of Satan? Why or why not?

Chapter Five

SATAN AND SELF-SACRIFICING LOVE

Get behind me, Satan!

—Mark 8:33

"Get behind me, Satan!" These are the scathing words Jesus spoke to Simon Peter as he talked with his disciples near the town of Caesarea Philippi (Mark 8:33).

What are we to make of Jesus' words? Was he suggesting that a supernatural evil power got into Peter? Some commentators have suggested this interpretation, but it seems more likely that Jesus used "Satan" in this passage as a metaphor for powerful temptation. He might have said, "Get away, Temptation!"

It was not a calm and quiet statement. And it was not simply a reprimand to Peter. We hear Jesus' agony and struggle in his exclamation, "Get behind me, Satan!" What temptation was so strong that Jesus addressed it as Satan?

Which Path to Choose?

In chapter 3, we saw that Jesus faced temptation in the wilderness before he began his public ministry. Now Jesus had come to another turning point in his life. Again he had to decide whether to follow the difficult way to which God called him or to choose an easier road.[1] According to all three of the Synoptic Gospels, Jesus' conversation with his disciples at Caesarea Philippi forms a transition between Jesus' ministry in his native Galilee and the beginning of his journey to Jerusalem and the cross (Matt. 16:13–23; Mark 8:27–33; Luke 9:18–22).[2]

In Galilee, Jesus had taught with authority, claimed the power to forgive sin, healed people who were sick, and performed many miracles including feeding a throng of thousands with a few loaves and fish. He had attracted huge crowds and won popular acclaim. Although he had begun to make enemies of Judaism's leaders, he was not yet posing a serious threat to them. If he had remained in the area around Galilee, Jesus probably could have continued to grow in popularity without challenging the power of Jewish authorities so strongly that they would seek to get rid of him.

At that moment in his ministry, Jesus had several options. He could remain silent. He could placate the religious authorities with compromise and soothing words. He could remain in the relative safety of Galilee. Or he could embark on a journey to Jerusalem, proclaiming the gospel all along the way.

Jerusalem was the city of the Temple, the center of Judaism. It was also the seat of political power. From Jerusalem, Herod administered Roman law throughout the region on behalf of the emperor. Jesus knew that going to Jerusalem would set him on a collision course with both Jewish and Roman authorities. It was a path that would almost certainly end in his death. The temptation to choose an easier way must have been very attractive.

All that was surely in Jesus' mind as he led his disciples north from Galilee to the region of Caesarea Philippi, an area that is now in the Golan Heights. Away from the crowds that followed him, Jesus spent some quiet time with his disciples. He talked about who he was and about what that meant. Perhaps he hoped for their support in the decision that he knew he must make.

"Who Do You Say that I Am?"

"Who do people say that I am?" Jesus asked his disciples. They answered that some said, "John the Baptist; and others, Elijah; and still others, one of the prophets." Then Jesus asked them, "But who do you say that I am?" Peter answered, "You are the Messiah" (Mark 8:27–29). The Hebrew word *Messiah*, translated *Christ* in Greek, means "anointed one." The Jews expected God to send a Messiah, a Christ, who would assume the throne of King David and restore to Israel the independence and political power it had known during David's reign. Could Jesus be this Christ? Peter was certain of it.

For Christians who are familiar with this story, Jesus' response to Peter's strong confession, "You are the Christ," probably comes to mind as it was recorded in the Gospel of Matthew. "Blessed are you, Simon son of Jonah! For flesh and blood has not revealed this to you, but my Father in heaven" (16:17).

The Gospel accounts of this story vary slightly, and Matthew's is the only one that contains these affirming words. But even in Matthew, the story moves quickly from affirmation to warning. Matthew, Mark, and Luke all agree that Jesus promptly ordered the disciples not to tell anyone that he was the Messiah.

Why did Jesus command the disciples not to tell anyone? Peter had spoken correctly. Why not proclaim the good news from the housetops?

The simple and obvious explanation is that Jesus did not want the disciples to tell people who he was because he realized they did not understand the words Peter had spoken. They did not know what it meant to be the Christ or to be Christ's followers. Jesus was saying, in effect, "You don't know what you are saying when you say that I am the Messiah, so don't talk about this yet."

The Christ Must Be Killed

Jesus then began to teach his disciples what it meant to be the Messiah. "From that time on, Jesus began to show his disciples that he must go to Jerusalem and undergo great suffering at the hands of the elders and chief priests and scribes, and be killed, and on the third day be raised" (Matt. 16:21). God's Christ could claim no easy path to victory. His road led to suffering and death. The concept of "Christ" could not be understood outside the context of the cross.

If Jesus had hoped for support from his closest friends for the decision he must make, he certainly did not get it. Peter protested! Suffering, rejection, and death were not what he had in mind! He rebuked Jesus for suggesting that those things would happen to him. Peter's protest gave words to the temptation that surely must have been in Jesus' heart, the temptation to turn his back on God's call rather than to walk the path of self-sacrificing love.

Jesus knew that God's way led to Jerusalem. If he were to proclaim the coming of God's reign where it would make the greatest impact on the most people, he had only one choice. If he were truly the Messiah, the Christ, he could not avoid Jerusalem. And so Jesus spoke directly to the voice of temptation, "Get behind me, Satan!" (Mark 8:33). I see Jesus' exclamation as an impassioned figure of speech rather than an implication that a supernatural power was at work in Peter. In the very next sentence, Jesus clarified his meaning, making no reference to the demonic, but telling Peter, "You are setting your mind not on divine things but on *human* things" (Mark 8:33, emphasis added).[3]

"You Are Setting Your Mind on Human Things"

Christian doctrine teaches that Jesus was human as well as divine. How human it would have been for Jesus to want to avoid the path that led to the cross!

How human it was for Peter to protest! The Jews did not expect their Messiah to die an ignominious death. They expected God's Anointed One to inflict suffering and death on Israel's enemies. How human it was for Peter to want to join in Jesus' victory without joining him in the cost.

How human it is for us to want to escape suffering, cost, rejection, and pain. How human it is to look for an easier way. We are tempted toward a self-centered faith, freely asking, What can Jesus do for me? but resisting the question, What is Christ's Spirit calling me to be and do?

We are tempted to view Christian faith in purely inner terms. We remember John 3:16: "For God so loved the world that he gave his only Son, so that everyone who believes in him may not perish but may have eternal life." And the words roll easily off our tongues: "Yes! I believe!" We may say, as Peter did, "You are the Christ!" Saying this makes us feel secure. We expect the affirmation, "Blessed are you . . . for flesh and blood has not revealed this to you." We are tempted to forget that the story does not end with these affirming words but that Jesus immediately corrected Peter's understanding of what it meant to acknowledge Jesus as the Christ and to follow him.

"Take Up Your Cross and Follow"

Jesus' words to his disciples as they set out on the journey to Jerusalem spelled out what it means to follow the Christ:

> If any want to become my followers, let them deny them-selves and take up their cross and follow me. (Matt. 16:24; Mark 8:34; Luke 9:23)

Those who want to save their life will lose it, and those

who lose their life for my sake will find it. (Matt. 16:25; Mark 8:35; Luke 9:24)

Whoever wants to be first must be last of all and servant of all. (Mark 9:35)

Unless you change and become like children, you will never enter the kingdom of heaven. Whoever becomes humble like [a] child is the greatest in the kingdom of heaven. (Matt. 18:3–4; Mark 10:15; Luke 18:17)

Whoever wishes to become great among you must be your servant, and whoever wishes to be first among you must be slave of all. For the Son of Man came not to be served but to serve, and to give his life a ransom for many. (Mark 10:43–45; Matt. 20:26–28)[4]

To all the voices of temptation that urge us to seek an easier road, the response of a true follower of the Christ must be, "Get behind me, Satan! Get away, Temptation!"

Confessing Jesus as the Christ means committing our whole lives to a journey of self-sacrificing love. To say, as Peter did, "You are the Christ," is not enough. Words and ritual are not enough. Even worship is not enough. There is no cost-free path to joy, fulfillment, and peace. The easy roads we are tempted to follow lead only to disappointment, destruction, and death. To claim glory without pain, righteousness without self-sacrificing love, eternal life without suffering is to exhibit false faith. To worship a "crossless Christ" is to worship an idol. And to sanctify this false religion by calling it faith in Jesus the Christ is evil. Jesus' words to Peter are directed to us too. "Get behind me, Satan! For you are setting your mind not on divine things but on human things."

Set Your Mind on Divine Things

Setting our minds on divine things means following Christ, even to the cross. It means praying as Jesus taught, "Thy will be done." It means committing our whole lives to the way of self-sacrificing love.

Jesus' teaching at Caesarea Philippi may sound like bad news. It did to Peter. Peter was so shaken by words such as "rejection" and "death" that he missed the good news. According to all three Synoptic Gospels, Jesus not only said he must suffer, be rejected, and be killed; he also said that after three days, he would rise again. Peter did not seem to hear that promise. He was too busy worrying about suffering and cost. Peter had his mind on human things, not on divine things.

When we cast aside the temptation to set our minds on human things and turn our spirits toward divine things, we hear good news. A road that leads to joy and life does exist. And we can choose that path. It is the way of self-sacrificing love. It passes through cost, pain, and even death. But it is the only way.

To Think About

1. In choosing the way that led to Jerusalem and the cross, Jesus resisted the temptation to choose an easier road, saying, "Get behind me, Satan!" Where do you think Jesus gained the strength to choose the way of the cross?

2. What hard choice are you facing right now? What choice do you believe God is calling you to make? How are you tempted to choose a different path?

3. Where can you find the strength to make the decision you truly believe is right for you?

4. Try picturing your greatest temptation as a person. Give it a name, such as "Satan," "Enemy," "Tempter," or a personal name

(but not the name of someone you know). How does it make a difference to personalize your temptation?

5. Do you see temptation as supernatural or as human? How does your answer to this question make a difference in your actions?

6. How are you setting your mind on divine things?

Chapter Six

SATAN AND THE
WORD

Satan immediately comes and takes away the word that is sown.

—Mark 4:15

The fourth and last mention of Satan that is common to the Synoptic Gospels occurs in the interpretation of Jesus' parable about a farmer. "A sower went out to sow," Jesus said. As the sower scattered seed, some fell on the path, and birds came and ate it up. Some fell on rocky ground where it did not have much soil; it sprang up quickly but since it had no root, it withered away. Some fell among thorns, and the thorns grew up and choked it. But other seed fell on good soil and brought forth grain, "growing up and increasing and yielding thirty and sixty and a hundredfold" (Mark 4:1–9; Matt. 13:1–9; Luke 8:4–8).

When the disciples did not understand the parable, Jesus explained its meaning: "The sower sows the word. These are the ones on the path where the word is sown: when they hear, Satan immediately comes and takes away the word that is sown in them." Other seeds are sown on rocky ground. When persecution arises, they quickly fall away. Others are sown among thorns; the cares of the world, the lure of wealth, and the desire for other things choke the Word and it yields nothing. The ones sown on good soil hear the Word, accept it, and bear fruit, "thirty and sixty and a hundredfold" (Mark 4:13–20; Matt. 13:18–23; Luke 8:11–15).

A Later Addition?

There is broad consensus among biblical scholars that Jesus' parable and his explanation of its meaning come from two different strands of the oral tradition. While the parable probably reflects the words of Jesus himself, the interpretation, with its mention of Satan, seems to date to the period of the post-Easter church.

Scholars base this conclusion on several observations. First, the language of the explanation is different from the style of the majority of Jesus' sayings. C. H. Dodd, in *The Parables of the Kingdom,* notes that the explanation in Mark 4:11–20 includes seven words that are not found in the rest of the Synoptic Gospels, and that all seven of these words are characteristic of the vocabulary of Paul and other later writers. He states, "These facts create at once a presumption that we have here not a part of the primitive tradition of the words of Jesus, but a piece of apostolic teaching."[1]

Second, the type of allegory found in the explanation of the parable was not typical of Jesus' teaching. Jesus often taught in parables, but he rarely used allegory. A parable makes a single comparison and its details do not have independent significance. In an allegory, each detail is a separate metaphor with a significance of its own. The original parable of the sower focused on a single message, as we will see. The allegorical interpretation, on the other hand, speaks of four kinds of hearers and assigns a specific meaning to each one. The birds who devoured the seed along the path symbolize Satan. Rocky soil represents shallow faith. Thorns stand for worldly values. Those sown in good soil are the ones who hear, understand, respond, and bear fruit. Jesus usually did not assign such specific meanings to the details of his stories.

A third reason scholars believe that the explanation of the parable comes from a later strand of tradition than the parable itself is that the central message of the parable is different from the central message of its allegorical interpretation. Although these messages are not in conflict with each other, they suggest that Jesus' original parable has been reinterpreted to address the circumstances of the early church, circumstances that included persecution and the lure of accumulated wealth. To understand the reference to Satan in the parable of the sower, we will find it helpful to look at the central message both of the original parable and of the later explanation of its meaning.

The Central Message of the Parable

In all three of the Synoptic Gospels, the parable of the sower is one of several parables that describe the coming reign of God. To paint a picture of God's coming reign, Jesus drew imagery from the everyday life of his listeners. "A sower went out to sow." A farmer scattering seed would have been a common sight in Jesus' day. In first-century Palestine, farmers did not plow a field to prepare it for planting. The sower tossed the seed by hand over the top of the ground, then plowed it into the soil. Jesus' hearers could easily picture seed falling on different kinds of earth, hard soil that had been beaten into a path, rocky soil with little moisture, soil choked with weeds. Such was the universal experience of those who planted seed and worked the ground. Not every seed would bear fruit. Planting inevitably involved some loss. Jesus gave three everyday examples of seed that failed to take hold and grow. He did not explore the reasons why a particular seed did not take root; instead he moved quickly to the central point of the parable. Some seed will fall on good ground, and it will produce "thirty and sixty and a hundredfold."

The quantity "thirty and sixty and a hundredfold" emphasizes the abundance of the harvest. It was no ordinary yield. John Dominic Crossan, in his book *In Parables,* explains that the point of the parable is to emphasize not growth, but miracle. It is not "organic and biological development but the gift-like nature, the graciousness and the surprise of the ordinary, the advent of bountiful harvest despite the losses of sowing. . . . It is like this that the Kingdom is in advent. It is surprise and it is gift."[2]

In all three of the Synoptic Gospels, the parable of the sower follows incidents in which Jesus' word has not been properly heard and therefore has failed to take root. In Matthew and Mark, the parable follows soon after the incident discussed in chapter 4, where some of those who watched Jesus heal a blind man accused him of casting out demons by the power of Satan. In Luke, it comes in the midst of increasing controversy over Jesus' actions, controversy that caused Jesus to compare people of his generation to children in the marketplace calling to one another:

We played the flute for you, and you did not dance;
we wailed, and you did not weep. (Luke 7:32)

The parable of the sower, as first told by Jesus, is a story of encouragement in the face of disappointment. The central question of the parable is, Will the effort to sow the seed of God's Word bear fruit? The parable of the sower is the first of a group of parables that answer the same question about the coming of God's reign.

The kingdom of God is as if someone would scatter seed on the ground, and would sleep and rise night and day, and the seed would sprout and grow, he does not know how. The earth produces of itself, first the stalk, then the head, then the full grain in the head. (Mark 4:26–28)

[The reign of God] is like a mustard seed, which, when sown upon the ground, is the smallest of all the seeds on earth; yet when it is sown it grows up and becomes the greatest of all shrubs, and puts forth large branches, so that the birds of the air can make nests in its shade. (Mark 4:31–32; Matt. 13:31–32; Luke 13:18–19)

The kingdom of heaven is like yeast that a woman took and mixed in with three measures of flour until all of it was leavened. (Matt. 13:33; Luke 13:20–21)

Will God's reign come? Jesus' answer is, "Yes! Do not be discouraged!" Despite its apparent insignificance and despite some losses, the Word of God, like the mustard seed, like the seed that grows of itself in the night, and like the seed that falls on good ground, will grow and bear fruit as much as a hundredfold. God's reign will come as both gift and miracle. The imperative of the parable is "Sow in faith!"

The Central Message of the Interpretation

The disciples did not understand the parable, and they asked Jesus to explain it. In the explanation, the emphasis shifts from the promise that the seeds of God's reign will bear abundant fruit to the responsibility of each hearer to listen and respond to the Word. The central question of the explanation is not, Will the sower's effort to sow the Word succeed? The central question is, What kind of hearer am I?

As Jesus explained the parable, he named four kinds of hearers and urged his followers to ask themselves, Am I like a hard path that the Word cannot penetrate, so that "Satan," the power of temptation, is able to steal the seed away? Am I rocky ground in which the Word grows up quickly but then withers in the face of persecution because it has no depth of soil? Am I ground choked with weeds? Or am I good soil in which the Word can grow and bear abundant fruit? To rephrase the message of the interpretation in today's idiom, we might say, "Listen up! Open your ears! Open your minds! Open your hearts! Pay attention! Respond!"

The Evil One

Within the general context of the commandment to cultivate good soil within our hearts so that we may hear and respond to God's Word, we come to the specific reference to Satan, or the Evil One.[3] Again we ask the question we have asked about each of the references to Satan in the Gospels: What does the Satan language in this story say to us about the power of evil in our lives?

Satan is not a central figure in this parable. The central figures are the sower and the hearers. Satan seems to be a rather casual addition to the story, an addition that suggests that in the early church "Satan" was a common way of referring to the power of temptation. Yet even though Satan does not play a central role in the story, the Satan language conveys a message about the power of evil in the lives of first-century Christians and in our lives today.

The interpretation of the parable stresses personal responsibility. Temptation is not a supernatural power that we are helpless to resist. Temptation has the power to steal the seed only when the soil is left uncultivated. Our choices determine whether or not we are "good soil." Our decisions can harden our hearts; they can produce shallow faith; they can nurture inner "thorns and weeds." Or they can foster growth. The responsibility for our choices, and for their consequences, is ours.

Looking more closely at the role of Satan in the interpretation of the parable, we may notice that the only seeds Satan steals are the ones along the path. Why were the seeds along the path particularly vulnerable?

A path is a place where the ground has been hardened by repeated traffic. A path is not made by a woman who loses her way once or twice or by a man who occasionally decides to take a shortcut. Earth becomes hardened into a path by repetition, persons walking the same way over and over again. The image suggests habits that harden our hearts.

A comparison to the story of Jesus' temptation in the wilderness seems relevant here. In chapter 3, we saw Jesus resist the power of the Tempter by calling on the resources of his faith, remembering the Scripture, quoting God's law, and turning his heart to God in obedience. In the discussion of that story, I suggested that the power to resist temptation comes, at least in part, through cultivating habits of faithfulness. In the Satan language of the parable of the sower, I see the flip side of this message, the same meaning stated in negative rather than positive terms. Cultivating habits of faithlessness makes us prey to the power of temptation. The ones along the path hear the Word, but "Satan immediately comes and takes away the word that is sown in them" (Mark 4:15). Unlike Jesus, who gained the power to resist temptation from cultivating habits of faithfulness, those who cultivate habits of *faithlessness* harden their hearts to God's Word.

What are the habits that harden our hearts to the Word of God, inviting temptation to steal away that Word? Habits of anger, hatred, and vengeance? Habits of self-centeredness? Habits of alcohol or drug abuse? Habits of intellectual or spiritual pride? Habits of using others for our personal gain? Habits of heedless pursuit of pleasure? Habits of chasing after wealth, power, or status? The parable's Satan language urges us to ask and to answer these questions.

Bear Fruit

Although Jesus' original parable of the sower and the later interpretation of that parable convey a slightly different message, the messages are closely related; one supports the other. Jesus' original parable brought encouraging news to those who wondered whether the seed scattered by the sower would bear fruit. The interpretation emphasized the hearers' responsibility to take the sower's word to their hearts and to respond by bearing fruit. God's reign will come as gift and miracle, but those who receive it must accept the gift. If we open our ears, our minds, and our hearts, if we pay attention to God's Word as it is proclaimed in the Gospels, the seed planted by God and nurtured by the Spirit of Christ will bear fruit, as much as a hundredfold.

To Think About

1. What is the "word" sown by the sower? If you were to try to summarize the "word," what five or six points would be most important to you?

2. Why did first-century Christians need to be assured that God's reign would come? Why do we need this assurance?

3. What habits may be hardening your inner soil?

4. What are "thorns" in your life that choke out the Word?

5. How would you rate the depth of your faith on a scale from 1 to 5, with 1 being "very deeply rooted," and 5 being "so shallow a slight breeze would blow it away"? What are some reasons for the rating you gave? How do you feel about where you rated yourself?

6. How are you cultivating good inner soil?

Part Three

SATAN IN THE NEW TESTAMENT CHURCH

Chapter Seven

SATAN AND
THE SPIRITUAL LIFE

The god of this world has blinded the minds of the unbelievers.
—2 Corinthians 4:4

Our study of the four references to Satan that are common to
more than one Synoptic Gospel has provided some insight into
Jesus' teaching about the power of evil in the world and in our
lives. Now we turn to the books of the New Testament that
describe the life and preaching of the early church.

The principal founder of the first Christian churches was
the apostle Paul. This devout Jew and former persecutor of
Christians, who had a dramatic conversion after seeing a vision
of the risen Christ, became the most effective missionary of early
Christianity. The letters he wrote to the churches he founded
make up a substantial portion of the New Testament. He had a
profound impact on the early church, and his influence on
Christian doctrine extends to our time. The writings of Paul,
therefore, are the obvious beginning point for our study of Satan
in the New Testament church.

Of the twenty-seven books in the New Testament, thirteen
are ascribed to Paul.[1] Of these, seven were almost certainly
written by the apostle himself, in the opinion of nearly all biblical scholars. They are Romans, First and Second Corinthians,
Galatians, Philippians, First Thessalonians, and Philemon. The
authorship of Ephesians, Colossians, and Second Thessalonians

is hotly debated. And most biblical scholars today have concluded that First and Second Timothy and Titus were written somewhat after Paul's time, perhaps by later disciples who were influenced by his teaching.[2]

One way to gain insight into Paul's understanding of Satan is to survey his writings. Before you read any farther, I suggest that you take a little time to conduct such a survey. Read quickly from Romans through Second Thessalonians, underlining every reference to Satan. Add Philemon and you will have covered all the Pauline letters, including the three whose authorship is debated. You can do this reading in just a few hours, and I think you will find it well worth your time.

Surveying the Pauline writings may produce some surprises, for the references to Satan are not as numerous as we might expect. The book of Romans, which comes closer than any of Paul's other letters to being a systematic statement of his theology, contains only one mention of Satan. Galatians and Philippians have none. First Thessalonians includes two. First Corinthians contains three. Second Corinthians has five.[3] If Satan were a foundational element of Paul's theology, we would expect to find more references. For the sake of comparison, Paul mentions sin more than fifty times, flesh more than eighty, and law more than one hundred.

The Flesh

In the vast majority of his works, Paul contrasted a life governed by the Spirit of Christ not with a life ruled by Satan, but with a life governed by the "flesh." Satan is not a foundational element in Paul's thought; the flesh clearly is. Before we can understand the role of Satan in Paul's works, we need to explore his concept of the flesh.

Paul sometimes used the "flesh" (Greek *sarx*) as a value-neutral synonym for the human body, but more often the flesh represents the seat of all lawless desires. The flesh consists of the baser human instincts and appetites, and it is not limited to the physical. The works of the flesh include not only fornication, impurity, licentiousness, drunkenness, and carousing, but also "idolatry, sorcery, enmities, strife, jealousy, anger, quarrels, dissensions, factions, envy" (Gal. 5:19–21). The flesh is opposed to the Spirit. Paul was not describing a dichotomy between body and mind; he saw a contest within each person between what is of God and what is hostile to God. The struggle is a matter of life and death. "To set the mind on the flesh is death, but to set the mind on the Spirit is life and peace" (Rom. 8:6).

Romans 5–7 contains Paul's most searching analysis of the relationship between the flesh and the Spirit. In chapter 5, Paul described the human situation before the coming of Christ. It was a time when "we were still weak" (v. 6), "we still were sinners" (v. 8), and "we were enemies" of God (v. 10).

The Weakness of the Flesh

The human condition, without the Spirit of Christ, is the flesh, a condition of weakness, sinfulness, and enmity toward God. Even the law, the commandments given to Moses, cannot free us from the flesh. The law is "holy and just and good," and it describes a life lived according to God's will (Rom. 7:12). Yet the law can become a "yoke of slavery" (Gal. 5:1). The law reveals our sinfulness to us and sets a standard no human being can fully attain. Even worse, the law can become an end in itself. We are tempted to use the law to try to earn "justification," Paul's term that means righteousness in God's eyes or right relationship with God. When we make the law an end in itself, when we use it to try to earn "justification," the law becomes a means toward our own selfish ends. Other people become objects, useful to us as we strive to overcome our anxiety about our righteousness. We "love" our neighbor to justify ourselves, not because we really care.[4] When the law becomes an end in itself, it is hostile to God.

Paul's picture of our human inability to save ourselves seems to grow out of his inner struggle. It reaches a poignant climax as he speaks personally about his predicament: "I can will what is right, but I cannot do it. . . . For I delight in the law of God in my inmost self, but I see in my members another law at war with the law of my mind, making me captive to the law of sin that dwells in my members. Wretched man that I am! Who will rescue me from this body of death?" (Rom. 7:18, 22–24).

Acting on our own, we cannot resist the temptations of the flesh. And although the law describes the ideal, it cannot equip us to attain it. We are "weak," "fearful," "wretched," "slaves," "captives," and "in bondage" to the powers of sin and death (Rom. 5:6, 8:15, 7:24, 6:6, 7:23, 8:21).

The Flesh and Satan

In Paul's penetrating analysis of the human condition in Romans 5–7, he did not mention Satan. Yet we can now see how the occasional references to Satan that appear in other parts of Paul's writing fit into the framework of his understanding of the human condition as *the flesh*. Satan was a concept that Paul's readers understood, and he used it to emphasize the weakness of the flesh against the power of evil. To do that, Paul portrayed Satan in a variety of roles.

1. In some instances, Satan is a synonym for *evil or temptation.*

I want you to be wise in what is good and guileless in what is evil. The God of peace will shortly crush Satan under your feet. (Rom. 16:19–20)

We wanted to come to you . . . but Satan blocked our way. (1 Thess. 2:18)

[Husbands and wives], do not deprive one another except perhaps by agreement for a set time, to devote yourselves to prayer, and then come together again, so that Satan may not tempt you because of your lack of self-control. (1 Cor. 7:5)

2. Another role for Satan is *teacher,* one whose lessons can lead persons to faith, or in the case of Paul himself, one who saved him from the sin of pride.

You are to hand this man [who had been living with his father's wife] over to Satan for the destruction of the flesh, so that his spirit may be saved in the day of the Lord. (1 Cor. 5:5)

To keep me [Paul] from being too elated, a thorn was given me in the flesh, a messenger of Satan to torment me, to keep me from being too elated. (2 Cor. 12:7)

Paul's representation of Satan as teacher was later picked up by the writer of First Timothy, who stated, "By rejecting conscience, certain persons have suffered shipwreck in the faith; among them are Hymenaeus and Alexander, whom I have turned over to Satan, so that they may learn not to blaspheme" (1:19–20). Satan's function here is close to the role of the satan in the Old Testament book of Job, where the satan acted as God's servant.

3. Occasionally, although only in books whose authorship has been debated, Satan appears as *God's antagonist in a cosmic battle between good and evil.*

Put on the whole armor of God, so that you may be able to stand against the wiles of the devil. For our struggle is not against enemies of blood and flesh, but against the rulers, against the authorities, against the cosmic powers of this present darkness, against the spiritual forces of evil in the heavenly places. (Eph. 6:11–12)

[The Day of God's Judgment] will not come unless the rebellion comes first and the lawless one is revealed, the one destined for destruction. . . . The coming of the lawless one is apparent in the working of Satan, who uses all power, signs, lying wonders, and every kind of wicked deception. (2 Thess. 2:3, 9–10)

The quotation from Second Thessalonians, just cited, addresses a question that had arisen in the church in Thessalonica. People were talking about the Day of God's Judgment, which by New Testament times had come to mean the time of God's victory in a cosmic battle over evil. This long-awaited day would bring final judgment and the inauguration of God's new age. Some of the Thessalonians were saying that God's day of judgment had already come. Second Thessalonians argued against this idea by saying that before the day came, the "lawless one" would be revealed. The precise identification of the "lawless one" is uncertain, but it is similar in meaning to the beast of Revelation, Christ's evil counterpart who acts with Satan's power in a cosmic battle between good and evil (Rev. 13). But a war in the heavens does not play a major role in Paul's letters, and it appears only in works whose authorship is questioned. Therefore, I will postpone a discussion of Satan's role in this cosmic battle until chapters 8 and 9, which deal with the book of Revelation.

4. Paul sometimes portrayed Satan as the *god of this world.*

The god of this world has blinded the minds of the unbelievers, to keep them from seeing the light of the gospel of
the glory of Christ. (2 Cor. 4:4, emphasis added)

You were dead through the trespasses and sins in which
you once lived, following the course of this world, following *the ruler of the power of the air,* the spirit that is now at
work among those who are disobedient. (Eph. 2:1–2,
emphasis added)

The "ruler of the power of the air" refers to the astrology of
Paul's day, which viewed the "air" as the lower atmosphere. In
contrast with the sky or the heavens, the air was the layer of
atmosphere closest to the earth. It was the place where evil spirits
dwelt, the domain from which they exerted their power over this
world.[5] The "ruler of the power of the air" and the "god of this
world" are two ways of saying the same thing. Both refer to Satan.

The concept of "god of this world" warrants more explo-
ration. Chapter 2 of this book showed that the idea of an evil
ruler of this world came into Jewish thought during the
intertestamental period in writings such as First Enoch and
Jubilees. People of Paul's day knew the stories of watcher angels
who rebelled against God by taking human wives and who,
under the leadership of an evil commander, variously called
Semjaza, Azazel, Mastema, or Satan, were expelled from heaven.
According to the legends, Semjaza/Azazel/Mastema/Satan eventually worked so much destruction that the whole earth fell
under the power of this Ruler of Evil.[6] In a few instances, Paul
drew on this imagery by referring to the "god of this world,"
meaning Satan.

This brief summary of four roles that Satan plays in Paul's letters makes it clear that Paul did not set forth a consistent doctrine of Satan. But in every case, Paul's mention of Satan emphasized the weakness of the flesh against the power of evil.

For me, and perhaps for you, Paul's analysis of the human situation is borne out in personal experience. I identify with Romans 7:18, "I can will what is right, but I cannot do it." And when I look at myself honestly, I can relate to Paul's exclamation of despair, "Wretched [person] that I am! Who will rescue me from this body of death?" (Rom. 7:24).

How can we free ourselves from the human condition that Paul described as the "flesh," "sin," "death," "slavery," "hostility to God," "wretchedness," and occasionally "the power of Satan"? Paul's answer was simple. We cannot. Fortunately, that is not the end of the story.

Divine Power

Although human beings alone are weak and enslaved to the flesh, we are *not* alone. Paul's desperate cry, "Who will rescue me from this body of death?" is followed by his exclamation, "Thanks be to God through Jesus Christ our Lord!" (Rom. 7:24–25).

The cornerstone of Paul's theology is his conviction that God in Christ has set us free from the flesh with its bondage to sin. In Christ, God has freed us from the power of evil, which is occasionally represented as "Satan." We cannot free ourselves; we cannot earn our "justification," right relationship with God. But we do not need to. God in Christ has done for us what we cannot do for ourselves. "God has done what the law, weakened by the flesh, could not do" (Rom. 8:3). No longer are we "slaves," "captives," and "in bondage" to sin and the flesh. "If anyone is in Christ, there is a new creation: everything old has passed away; see, everything has become new!" (2 Cor. 5:17).

Paul's letters are an ardent invitation to the spiritual life. They urge us to set our minds on the Spirit, accepting the gift of freedom from sin that God holds out to us. Paul assures us that not flesh, sin, evil, or "Satan" holds any power over us when we allow our lives to be filled with the Spirit. "You are not in the flesh; you are in the Spirit, since the Spirit of God dwells in you" (Rom. 8:9).

To Think About

1. Before you began reading this book, how would you have described the role of Satan in the letters of Paul? What insights have you gained from reading this chapter?

2. Can you identify with Paul's words in Romans 7:18: "I can will what is right, but I cannot do it"? Give some examples.

3. What forces within you seem to hold you "captive" or "slave"? How are mistakes from the past holding you in "bondage" in ways that affect your present and your future?

4. Paul did not believe that the law can save us from the condition that he described as "the flesh," "sin," and "evil" (which he sometimes also described as "Satan"). Do you agree? Why or why not?

5. Paul said, "You are not in the flesh; you are in the Spirit, since the Spirit of God dwells in you" (Rom. 8:9). How is this (or could this become) a reality in your life?

Chapter Eight

SATAN AND HOPE

*The great dragon was thrown down, that ancient
serpent, who is called the Devil and Satan, the deceiver of
the whole world—he was thrown down to the earth.*

—Revelation 12:9

The Bible's most quoted references to Satan appear in its last book,
the Apocalypse to John, more commonly known as Revelation.
(The Greek word *apokalypsis* means "revelation.") Satan the serpent, the dragon, the beast, the number 666, the star who fell
from heaven, the one who will be bound for a thousand years and
then released to lead the nations in battle against God—all these
are found in Revelation. Although other New Testament books
such as First Timothy, James, and First Peter also refer to Satan,
these references are not frequent, nor is the role of Satan substan-
tially different from the various roles Satan played in Paul's letters.
In Revelation, however, Satan becomes a central figure.

Revelation's symbolic language and fantastic imagery have
caught the imaginations of generation after generation, and its
readers have puzzled over their meaning. Through the centuries,
many Christians have interpreted Revelation as a prediction of
specific future events and have attempted to apply these "predictions" to happenings in their own time. M. Eugene Boring, in
his very helpful commentary on Revelation in the *Interpretation
Bible Commentary,* observes that those who take this approach to
Revelation typically see themselves as living in the last period
predicted, and they assign some of Revelation's symbols of evil

to persons or ideas of their own age. During the time of Martin Luther, for example, Protestant interpreters often saw the papacy symbolized by the "beast" of Revelation 13; Roman Catholics, in turn, found ways to make the name Martin Luther equal 666, Satan's "code name" in Revelation 13:18.[1] Some interpretations written during the Cold War equated the armies of Satan with the Soviet Union.

The problem with any theory that interprets Revelation as a prediction of specific events many centuries after the date of its writing is that it ignores the fact that Revelation was a letter written to a particular group of people who faced a specific crisis. This letter would have meant nothing to its first-century readers if its primary purpose were to predict events two thousand years into the future. A majority of contemporary scholars believe that a valid interpretation of Revelation, like an analysis of any other book of the Bible, should determine its meaning for its original hearers before applying it to life today. That is the approach I will follow as I attempt to make sense out of Satan's role in the Bible's last book. What message did this letter proclaim to the Christian church as it moved toward the end of the first century?

John of Patmos

On the tiny island of Patmos in the Aegean Sea, a man named John experienced an apocalypse, a revelation. He recorded his vision in a letter addressed to the seven churches of "Asia," the name then given to the Roman province located in the area that is now Turkey. The time was around 95, near the end of the reign of the Roman emperor Domitian.[2]

Who was this John? We do not know. He does not seem to be the same John who is associated with the Fourth Gospel.[3] All we know for sure about him is that he was banished from Asia to Patmos because he was a Christian (Rev. 1:9).

Christianity had developed a strong foothold in Asia in the cities of Ephesus, Smyrna, Pergamum, Thyatira, Sardis, Philadelphia, and Laodicea as a result of Paul's missionary journeys. And after the Romans crushed a Jewish rebellion in Palestine in 66–70, large numbers of Jews and Christians migrated to Asia seeking a more tolerant social and religious climate. To their disappointment, Christians discovered that life was not always better in Asia than it had been in Jerusalem. The Roman emperor Domitian, who ruled from 81 to 96, demanded that his subjects address him as "Lord and God." For most Roman subjects, the requirement to worship the emperor posed no threat; they merely added another god to the list of gods they already worshiped. But for Christians and Jews, who were commanded to have no other gods save the one God, the ruling precipitated a crisis. The Jews, who had a long and established history, managed to work out an agreement with the Romans whereby they were required to pray for the emperor but not to worship him.[4] But Christians, being a new and little-known sect and one that attracted primarily the lower classes, received no such indulgence from the Roman government. Christians who refused to worship the emperor could be punished by exile and even death.

Domitian exiled his own niece Domitilla, who almost certainly was a Christian, for "atheism," that is, for refusing to worship the emperor as Master and God.[5] Revelation mentions one Christian martyr, Antipas of Pergamum (2:13). And John himself had been exiled to Patmos for his Christian belief. The persecution of Christians under Domitian, however, appears to have been more spasmodic than systematic. Historians have not found evidence of organized oppression of Christians under Domitian. But John, who knew persecution firsthand, clearly expected his experience to become the norm for Christians in the near future. The *expectation* of a widespread reign of terror forms the historical backdrop of Revelation. John's apocalypse offered comfort and hope to those who expected to face exile, suffering, and even death for their Christian beliefs.

An Apocalyptic Response

First-century listeners, familiar with the Old Testament and with Jewish literature written during the period between the testaments, would have recognized Revelation as belonging to the type of literature called apocalyptic. Chapter 2 of this book explored the roots of Jewish apocalyptic literature and looked at some important examples. I suggest taking a few minutes to review that chapter, for much of the imagery that was introduced there appears again in Revelation. Christians of New Testament times would have heard in Revelation echoes of Isaiah, Ezekiel, Daniel, First Enoch, and Jubilees.[6] They would also have known other apocalyptic works such as Second Esdras in the Apocrypha, which was written about the same time as Revelation but was not accepted into the New Testament canon.

Apocalyptic literature was concerned with end times, the culmination of human history. This type of writing flourished during periods of crisis because it reassured the faithful that God controlled human destiny and that their present suffering would be brief. Daniel was written when Jews were being persecuted by the Greek emperor Antiochus Epiphanes. The Book of Watchers (later to become First Enoch), Jubilees, and other apocalyptic writings of the intertestamental period arose out of the struggle of orthodox Jews to preserve their faith and tradition against the threat of the attractive ideas and lifestyle of their Greek conquerors. Revelation was written by a Christian who had been exiled for refusing to worship the Roman emperor. For John of Patmos, as for earlier visionaries, unjust persecution raised faith questions. Why is a good and all-powerful God allowing us to suffer for our faithfulness? Will God help us? *Can* God help us? Will God's justice be done? Apocalypticism offered an answer.

As I noted in chapter 2, apocalyptic literature attempted to set the author's present sufferings within the framework of the whole span of human history. Apocalyptic visionaries understood all history as part of a cosmic battle between supernatural forces of good and evil. They believed that God was leading human history toward an end that God had already determined, and that the end had now been revealed in a vision. The vision, which usually included fantastic imagery, disclosed that the tribulation of the author's time signaled the beginning of the end of history. Current suffering would escalate as the end drew near, but the intensification would be a sign that God's new age was approaching. God's ultimate victory was certain. Jews, and later Christians, needed only to remain faithful until the day arrived.

Revelation follows this traditional apocalyptic pattern. In the first three chapters, John is directed in a vision to write letters to seven churches of Asia. In straightforward language, the letters address the present situation of Christians in Ephesus, Smyrna, Pergamum, Thyatira, Sardis, Philadelphia, and Laodicea. The letters praise the churches' faithfulness, chastise their sin, warn that all persons will be judged according to their works, and call Christians to remain steadfast in faith during the coming difficult days.

In chapter 4, the fantastic imagery begins. Chapters 4 to 18 present the sweep of history in vivid word pictures, describing in symbolic language the tribulation that signals the beginning of the end. Chapters 19 to 22 portray God's final victory in the battle between God and the forces of evil.

Satan is a prominent figure in this drama. A supernatural ruler of evil is not an essential characteristic of apocalyptic writing. As we noticed in chapter 2, Satan did not appear in the Old Testament book of Daniel. But much of the apocalyptic literature written between the testaments featured a supernatural ruler of evil whose names included Semjaza, Azazel, Mastema, and Satan. In Revelation, Satan plays a major role.

Because the Bible's last book is complex and confusing and because it contains so much of the imagery on which many current interpretations (and misinterpretations!) of Satan's role are based, I will devote two chapters to Revelation. This chapter will explore Satan's role in the escalating tribulation as the end draws near. The next chapter will look at the final confrontation between good and evil.

A Drama in Heaven

John's description of Satan's activities on earth is centered in Revelation 12–14, a section Dr. Boring describes as "the central axis of the book and the core of its pictorial argument."[7] In the visions that have led up to this point, John has seen a heavenly throne and One seated upon it who holds a scroll sealed with seven seals. A "Lamb standing as if it had been slaughtered" (5:6) opens the seals, and each one introduces an earthly catastrophe. The seventh seal reveals seven trumpets given to seven angels, each bringing a new plague upon the earth. The seventh trumpet announces the consummation of history and the coming of the new age.

As chapter 12 begins, we expect the action to move rapidly to the final confrontation between good and evil. But that does not happen. Instead, chapters 12 to 14 break the sequences of sevens. The formula will pick up again in chapter 16 when seven bowls spill out more woes. But the visions of chapters 12 to 14 step aside from this rhythm in order to view the happenings on earth from the perspective of heaven. The drama taking place in heaven is the key to understanding what is happening on earth.[8]

The first character who appears in the heavenly drama is a woman, "clothed with the sun, with the moon under her feet, and on her head a crown of twelve stars" (12:1). She is pregnant, and she cries out in birth pangs, evoking for the hearer the image of Mary. As the story continues, we will find that the woman is a heavenly representative not just of Mary, but of the whole people of Israel, from whom the Messiah was born. Eventually, she will come to represent the "new Israel," the Christian church.

The Dragon Who Is the Devil and Satan

Another character enters, "a great red dragon, with seven heads and ten horns, and seven diadems on his heads" (12:3). John identifies this dragon as "that ancient serpent, who is called the Devil and Satan" (12:9). Throughout Revelation, John draws on Old Testament imagery and on myths that were familiar to his hearers. He does not strive for consistency; he is not making a systematic and analytical argument. He flashes one mental snapshot after another upon the readers' imagination to evoke a cumulative emotional response.

Through imagery, John connects Satan with at least five biblical or mythological images that would have been known to his hearers. (1) Satan is the serpent of the Garden of Eden. (2) Satan is the primordial dragon mentioned in the Old Testament, which in Canaanite mythology was the seven-headed monster Sea, destroyed by the god Baal in order to establish his authority over the earth.[9] (3) Satan is the dragonlike beast with ten horns of Daniel 7:7, which in Daniel represented the Greek Empire. (4) Satan is the star that had fallen from heaven to earth of Isaiah 14, which in Isaiah referred to the arrogant king of Babylon. Isaiah had poked fun at Israel's enemy by calling him "Day Star," the Canaanite god who was expelled from heaven and forced to rule on earth after making an unsuccessful attempt to replace the god

Baal.[10] (5) As a star fallen from heaven, Satan would also have reminded first-century readers of the watcher angels who, according to the Book of Watchers, Jubilees, and other intertestamental literature, rebelled against God under the leadership of a ruler of evil and were banished to earth where they continued to work destruction.[11] In Revelation, John gathers all these familiar symbols of evil into the figure of Satan.

As the heavenly drama continues in Revelation 12, the dragon, which is the Devil and Satan, hovers over the woman, intending to devour the child as soon as it is born. But the child, a son who is to rule all nations, is "snatched away and taken to God" (12:5). In this brief sentence, John represents the life, death, and resurrection of Jesus.[12] The woman flees into the wilderness where she is to be protected and nourished by God during the coming period of tribulation.

Satan Thrown Down to Earth

Then war breaks out in heaven. The archangel Michael, Israel's patron saint, defeats the dragon and the dragon's angels, and they can no longer remain in heaven. The great dragon is thrown down, "that ancient serpent, who is called the Devil and Satan, the deceiver of the whole world"; the dragon is "thrown down to the earth." And the dragon's angels are thrown down with the dragon (12:7–9). Then John hears a voice in heaven, proclaiming, "Now have come the salvation and the power and the kingdom of our God and the authority of his Messiah, for the accuser of our comrades has been thrown down. . . . They have conquered him by the blood of the Lamb" (12:10–11). Satan has been defeated in heaven. While Michael has apparently been a participant in the battle, the decisive action in Satan's defeat is Christ's death on the cross. Satan is conquered *by the blood of the Lamb.*

The time of Satan's expulsion from heaven will be confusing if we try to turn John's imagery into an explanation of the origin of evil. The primordial dragon of Near Eastern mythology was defeated before the creation of the earth. The watcher angels rebelled against heaven after the time of Adam and Eve, when people were beginning to multiply on the earth.[13] Yet Revelation 12:10 clearly states that the time of Satan's expulsion from heaven is "now." The time of Satan's defeat in heaven is the first century, both the time of the crucifixion of Jesus and the time of John's vision, for Satan is conquered by the blood of the Lamb *and* by the testimony of Christian martyrs (12:11). Inconsistencies about the time of Satan's "fall to earth" are a problem only if we attempt to find answers in Revelation to questions that the churches of Asia never asked. The first-century Christians who were facing persecution were not concerned about the origin of evil. They were asking about God's faithfulness, God's justice, and God's power to correct the terrible unfairness of their situation. John's revelation was intended to give them the hope that would enable them to hold on to their faith in the midst of crisis. Thus, John assured them that their present tribulation was a sign that Satan had been defeated in heaven and thrown down to earth.

As the story continues, the dragon (Satan), enraged by defeat and by the shortness of time left on earth, pursues the woman who gave birth to the male child. When even the earth comes to her protection, the dragon is furious with the woman and goes off to make war on the rest of her children, who represent the Christian church, "those who keep the commandments of God and hold the testimony of Jesus" (12:13–18). Through imagery and allusion, John has presented a picture of an evil so large that it encompasses every known symbol of evil. And to that portrait John now adds the figures of Satan's agents, the beast and the false prophet.

Satan's Agents

As the dragon takes a stand on the shore, John sees a beast with seven heads and ten horns rising out of the sea. This beast is an evil counterpart to Christ; it is the earthly incarnation of Satan the dragon as Jesus was the earthly incarnation of God. "The dragon gave [the beast] his power and his throne and great authority" (13:2). For this reason, the beast is sometimes referred to as antichrist, although this name does not appear in Revelation.

The beast from the sea would have evoked the image of the Roman Empire to first-century hearers, whose land had been conquered by Romans arriving from the sea. The seven heads symbolized the seven Roman emperors, a connection that John makes specific in 17:9–10 where the seven heads correspond both to the seven hills of Rome and to seven Roman kings. One of the heads seems to have received a deathblow, but its mortal wound has been healed. This refers to a well-known rumor that the hated Roman emperor Nero, who had committed suicide, had been restored to life and would one day return to lead an army against the Roman Empire.[14] The beast also clearly refers to the last beast in the book of Daniel, which had ten horns representing ten Greek emperors, with the final horn representing the hated Antiochus Epiphanes. By John's time, Jews had often reinterpreted this beast to signify the Roman Empire.[15] Clearly, the beast from the sea evoked the image of Rome for John's hearers. In a larger sense, however, it represents the arrogance and corruption of all political power.

As the vision continues, John sees a second beast, this one rising out of the earth. John identifies this beast as a false prophet who promotes the worship of the dragon and the beast (19:20; 20:10). Who was this beast from the land, the false prophet? John declares, "Let anyone with understanding calculate the number of the beast, for it is the number of a person. Its number is six hundred sixty-six" (13:18). The number 666 may simply represent imperfection. Since seven represented perfection, six or a combination of sixes would always fall short of perfection. But the number very likely has a more precise meaning. In John's time, each letter of the alphabet was represented by a number, and the number of a word would be the sum of the value of each of its letters. Many scholars believe that the sum of the numbers 666 equals the name Nero, the infamous Roman emperor who persecuted Christians. The letters "Neron Caesar" in the Hebrew spelling add up to 666.[16] Whoever John had in mind when he wrote the number 666, the false prophet also has a broader significance. It represents anyone who uses authority and power to mislead, corrupt, and champion false gods.

The Response of Faithful Christians

How were Christians who lived during the reign of the Roman emperor Domitian to respond to the forces of evil, which in those days seemed to be clothed in the garments of the Roman government? John's answer was unhesitating. Endure and have faith!

The forces of evil must have seemed all-powerful to Christians who lived at the mercy of Rome. For them, refusing to bow down to the emperor could mean exile or worse. Acknowledging Christ could mean death. It must have seemed to Christians that the only way to get along was to go along with the power structure of the day. But Revelation assured Christians that the apparent victory of evil was an illusion. Satan had already been conquered in heaven by the blood of the Lamb. To buy into the religion and the value system of the Roman Empire would be to follow a commander who had already been defeated. God and the Lamb would triumph on earth very soon, as they had already triumphed in heaven. Then the current injustice would be corrected. The faithful would be rewarded. Those who worshiped the beast would drink the wine of God's wrath and be "tormented with fire and sulfur in the presence of the holy angels and in the presence of the Lamb" (14:9–10).

Modern Christians may find John's picture of eternal damnation disturbing. Where is the God of mercy and forgiveness? What about the suggestion found in the rest of the New Testament, and even in other parts of Revelation, that Jesus came as a savior for *all* humankind?[17] But to raise these questions is to press John's impressionistic and pictorial language for a statement of doctrine that John did not attempt. Revelation was not intended to describe the fate of non-Christians; it was meant to encourage believers to remain faithful. John's purpose was to bring hope to Christians in a time of hopelessness, to bolster their courage, to strengthen their faith, and to assure them that despite their apparent helplessness, victory belonged to Christ and to those who followed him, even when they followed him unto death.

"Here is a call for the endurance and faith of the saints," John proclaimed (13:10). Death would not have the final word! "Blessed are the dead who from now on die in the Lord. . . . They will rest from their labors, for their deeds follow them" (14:13). Have faith and endure!

For us who live at the dawn of the twenty-first century, the book of Revelation continues to hold fascination and to speak with power. Evil is as real today as it was in the first century, and we have some of the same questions that troubled Revelation's first readers. How are we to respond to suprapersonal forces of evil, evil that seems larger than human sin? Should we go along in order to get along? Is good stronger than evil? Is God really at work in our world, or are we alone in the struggle against institutionalized injustice, personal sin, and overwhelming temptation? Where do we find help in the midst of crisis? Where do we find hope in the midst of hopelessness?

As we ask and attempt to answer these questions, John's pictorial language still speaks with relevance and power.

Great and amazing are your deeds, Lord God the Almighty!
Just and true are your ways, King of the nations!
Lord, who will not fear and glorify your name?
For you alone are holy.
   All nations will come and worship before you,
for your judgments have been revealed. (15:3–4)

To Think About

1. What parallels do you see between the circumstances of first-century Christians living under Roman domination and the situation of Christians today? What differences do you see?

2. What are forces of evil in our society today? If you were to portray them in symbolic language, what faces would they wear?

3. John of Patmos believed that the only options for the Christians to whom his letter was addressed were to sell out to Roman values or to die for their faith. What are our options? What are the costs of faithfulness today?

4. When have you felt, or do you feel, that the struggle against evil is hopeless? What causes you to feel this way?

5. According to Revelation, what was the source of hope for faithful Christians who faced persecution? What are your sources of hope? Why is hope important?

6. Revelation asserts that in Jesus' life, death, and resurrection, God has already won the victory over evil. What do Christ's life, death, and resurrection mean for you and for your life?

Chapter Nine

SATAN AND THE ARMIES
OF HEAVEN

*Satan . . . will come out to deceive the nations at the four
corners of the earth, . . . to gather them for battle.*

—Revelation 20:7–8

In the closing chapters of Revelation, we come at last to the
final confrontation between God and the forces of evil. These
chapters have inspired many imaginative interpretations over
the last nineteen centuries, from Dante's *Inferno* to Milton's
Paradise Lost to Hal Lindsey's *The Late Great Planet Earth* to a
plethora of millennial theories that attempt to relate John's
visions to events taking place at the turn of the twenty-first century. Biblical interpreters in many time periods have found
"proof" in Revelation that they were living in the final years of
human history.

Throughout this book, I have suggested that a valid interpretation of any scripture must attempt to determine its meaning for its original hearers. Before reading farther, take a
moment to imagine yourself as a member of the church of
Ephesus, Pergamum, or Laodicea in the year 95, near the end
of the reign of the Roman emperor Domitian. What questions
might you have about God's power, justice, and faithfulness as
you face the threat of a terrible wave of persecution? Try to listen with the ears of a first-century Christian as John of Patmos
describes the events that he believes will lead to the end of
human history.

The Amassment of Forces

As John's visions continue, he sees seven angels pour out seven bowls of wrath upon the earth, and evil spirits like frogs spew forth from the mouths of the dragon, the beast, and the false prophet. These evil spirits assemble the armies of the rulers of the whole world for combat at Armageddon on the "great day of God the Almighty" (16:13–14, 16). The location of Armageddon is uncertain, but it may be an allusion to Megiddo, which had been the site of several decisive battles in Israel's history.[1]

Awaiting the beginning of the conflagration, John foresees God's judgment on "Babylon," clearly a metaphor for Rome. Babylon, "mother of whores and of earth's abominations," is "drunk with the blood of the saints." She is seated upon "a scarlet beast" with seven heads and ten horns (17:3, 5–7). As often happens in John's imagery, this scarlet beast represents several layers of meaning at once. It is Satan's agent, the beast, to whom Satan has granted power and authority (13:2). It is Leviathan, the sea monster we met in chapters 1 and 8 of this book.[2] And the beast also represents Rome. Its seven heads stand for the seven hills of Rome, and its horns represent emperors. The image, if we try to picture it as it is described, boggles the imagination. Both the beast and the woman who rides upon it represent Rome! But John's meaning is clear. The rulers of the world have "committed fornication" with Rome; that is, they have worshiped Rome, its gods, its emperor, and its way of life (17:2). In so doing, the world's rulers have "united in yielding their power and authority to the beast" (17:13). Now, led by the beast, the nations gather to make war on the Lamb.

The long-awaited battle, which the preceding visions have previewed and foreshadowed, is finally to begin. John predicts its outcome with confidence: "The Lamb will conquer them, for he is Lord of lords and King of kings" (17:14). Funeral dirges for

"Babylon" are sung in heaven and on earth, and a multitude in heaven sings praises for God's coming victory (18:1–19:10). "Hallelujah!" they proclaim. "The marriage of the Lamb has come, and his bride has made herself ready" (19:6–7). The struggle between God and Satan approaches its apocalyptic climax.

The Lamb's Triumphal Entrance

As the confrontation begins, John sees heaven open, and a white horse appears. Its rider is called "Faithful and True, and in righteousness he judges and makes war. . . . He is clothed in a robe dipped in blood" (19:11–13). Understanding this figure of the Lamb is vital for our interpretation of the entire book of Revelation.

The Lamb was introduced at the beginning of John's heavenly visions when John was transported to the throne of the Divine (4:2). The One seated on the divine throne had a scroll sealed with seven seals, and John began to weep because no one was found worthy to open the scroll. Then one of the elders who surrounded the divine throne said to John, "Do not weep. See, the Lion of the tribe of Judah, the Root of David, has conquered, so that he can open the scroll and its seven seals" (5:5). The "Lion of the tribe of Judah" clearly referred to the Messiah. Old Testament and intertestamental literature had portrayed the expected Messiah as a lion (Gen. 49:9–10; Testament of Judah 24:5).[3] A "Root of David," a descendant of David, would come as a mighty lion to vanquish Israel's enemies. John had thus set the scene for the entrance of the Messiah, the only One qualified to open the seven seals.

But when the Messiah entered, he was not a lion at all! He was a Lamb, "standing as if it had been slaughtered" (5:6). This transformation of imagery from the lion into the slaughtered lamb is critical for an understanding of John's theology throughout Revelation and for interpreting the role of the Lamb in the final confrontation with the armies of Satan.[4] Lambs do not slaughter their enemies. They are meek and gentle creatures. More important, in the history of Israel, lambs were animals of sacrifice. The slaughtered lamb of Revelation brings to mind the Passover lamb of Exodus whose blood spared the firstborn of Israel from death while the firstborn of the Egyptians were killed (Exod. 11–13).[5] And in New Testament theology, framed in the words of the Gospel of John, "the Lamb of God who takes away the sin of the world" is Jesus (1:29).

Now, in Revelation 19, the Lamb, clearly symbolizing Christ, enters for the final confrontation with Satan, clothed in "a robe dipped in blood" (19:13). It is not the blood of Israel's enemies; the Lamb's robe is dipped in his own blood.[6] Throughout Revelation, John has insisted that Jesus the Christ triumphed not by killing his foes, but through his own death. In Revelation, the expected "Lion of the tribe of Judah" has become the sacrificial Lamb.

The Armies of Heaven

The slaughtered Lamb, entering the stage of human history for the final confrontation with evil, is followed by the "armies of heaven." These are Christian martyrs who, faithful unto death, have now joined Christ (7:13–17). Although they are described as armies, they are not dressed in battle gear; they are dressed for a wedding! "The armies of heaven, wearing fine linen, white and pure, were following [the Lamb] on white horses" (19:14). In the verses that preceded the confrontation, a multitude in heaven sang hymns celebrating God's coming victory and announcing the marriage of the Lamb: "For the marriage of the Lamb has come, and his bride has made herself ready; to her it has been granted to be clothed with fine linen, bright and pure" (19:7–8).

Now the armies of heaven—Christ's bride—present themselves for the wedding. They take no part in the battle itself.
They have no swords or guns; they are not backed by nuclear
arms. Any interpretation that sees in Revelation a call to become
part of "God's army" by amassing weapons for a final cataclysmic battle misrepresents the biblical text. The role of the
armies of heaven is to *celebrate the victory* of the Lamb, which
has already been accomplished through Jesus' life, death, and
resurrection and which is now to come to its full consummation.
Dressed in white, they present themselves for their union with
Christ the Lamb.

The Battle

John sees "the beast and the kings of the earth" gathered with
their armies to "make war against the rider on the horse and
against his army" (19:19). The Lamb's only weapon is a sharp
sword coming from his mouth (19:21). His battle instrument is
the *Word* of God. That and that alone. It is sufficient. After
nineteen chapters of buildup, John describes the battle with
Satan's agents, the beast and the false prophet, in one sentence:
"And the beast was captured, and with it the false prophet who
had performed in its presence the signs by which he deceived
those who had received the mark of the beast and those who
worshiped its image" (19:20). The victory is accomplished by
the sacrificial death of the Lamb whose sole weapon is God's
Word. The only way the followers of Christ are to participate in
the "battle" is to follow in the way of the Lamb, the incarnate
Word, even unto death.

The victory won, the beast and the false prophet are quickly
thrown into the "lake of fire that burns with sulfur" (19:20).
The reign of the idolatrous Roman Empire and all the nations
that gave themselves over to its power has ended.

The Binding of Satan

With Satan's agents destroyed, only the dragon remains. John sees an angel coming down from heaven who seizes "the dragon, that ancient serpent, who is the Devil and Satan," binds the dragon for a thousand years, throws it into a pit, locks it, and seals the pit so that Satan can deceive the nations no more, "until the thousand years [are] ended. After that he must be let out for a little while" (20:2–3). During this millennial period, the "souls of those who had been beheaded for their testimony to Jesus and for the word of God" will descend from heaven to earth and rule with Christ (20:4). (Notice that John never suggested that anyone would escape death. Apparently, he believed that all faithful Christians would be martyred in the coming persecution.)

The picture of the "binding" of Satan for a millennial period of one thousand years did not originate with John. It was part of a tradition he inherited from earlier Jewish and Christian writings.[7] Speaking of the coming of the great Day of God's Judgment when God would conquer Israel's enemies, Isaiah stated,

> On that day the Lord will punish
>> the host of heaven in heaven,
>> and on earth the kings of the earth.
> They will be gathered together
>> *like prisoners in a pit;*
> *they will be shut up in a prison,*
>> *and after many days they will be punished.* (Isa. 24:21–22, emphasis added)

As we saw in chapter 2 of this book, John and his readers were also familiar with legends of watcher angels who, under the leadership of a demonic leader variously named Semjaza, Azazel,

Mastema, and Satan, rebelled against God and corrupted the whole earth. First Enoch, where some of these stories are collected, tells how an angry God bound these evil angels "till the time when their guilt should be consummated, even for ten thousand years" (1 Enoch 18:11–16).[8] Second Peter, probably written somewhat later than Revelation, also referred to this common myth, saying that God did not spare the angels when they sinned, and committed them to chains of deepest darkness to be kept until the Judgment (2 Pet. 2:4).

Dr. Boring suggests that John's vision of a millennial period during which Satan will be bound and Christ will rule on earth brings together two different understandings of the ultimate goal of human history.[9] Most of the Old Testament prophets expected God's future reign to take place on this earth. With the rise of apocalypticism during the period between the testaments, however, and in the face of persecution, Jews and eventually Christians began to despair of the possibility of the redemption of this world. Their hope began to turn to a future beyond human history—a new age, a new earth, and a new Jerusalem. John's vision encompasses both ideas. For a "thousand years," which may represent an almost infinite period rather than a specific number, Christ will reign on earth. But ultimately, this world will end. Satan will be released for one last battle; then God will usher in a whole new age.

Perhaps another reason John portrays Satan as "bound" rather than as totally destroyed is that he is drawing his story line for this part of Revelation from Ezekiel 37–39. In Ezekiel 37, the prophet saw a valley of dry bones, which represented the people of Israel in exile in Babylon, where they were walking corpses, devoid of hope. In Ezekiel's vision, the Spirit of God put flesh on the dry bones and promised to bring the restored nation back to its own land to dwell with God forever (37:21, 27).

John's vision of a millennial period when Satan is bound and the earth is governed by Christ and the resurrected Christian martyrs corresponds to Ezekiel's vision of dry bones, raised from death to dwell with God. It would make a good ending to the story. But Ezekiel is not finished with evil. And John is not finished with Satan,

Satan, Gog, and Magog

Ezekiel 38 introduces a new crisis: "The word of the Lord came to me: Mortal, set your face toward Gog, of the land of Magog. . . . I am against you, O Gog . . . I will lead you out with all your army, horses and horsemen, all of them clothed in full armor. . . . In the latter years you shall go against a land restored from war, a land where people were gathered from many nations on the mountains of Israel" (Ezek. 38:1–8). Scholars have long speculated about the identity of the ruler Gog and his nation Magog without coming to any definitive conclusions. The best guess seems to be that Magog was a grandiose surrogate for Babylon, since Ezekiel speaks of the ruler Gog as a foe who would come out of the remotest parts of the north and Babylon was Israel's archfoe from the north.[10]

Following Ezekiel's story line, John announces, "When the thousand years are ended, Satan will be released from his prison and will come out to deceive the nations at the four corners of the earth, Gog and Magog, in order to gather them for battle; they are as numerous as the sands of the sea" (20:7–8).[11] "The nations," in the Old Testament, usually means pagan nations, nations that did not worship the God of Israel (Exod. 34:24; Deut 11:23; Pss. 9:19–20; 22:27; Isa. 14:9). Now Satan incites "the nations," represented by "Gog and Magog," to battle against God's people. "They marched up over the breadth of the earth and surrounded the camp of the saints and the beloved city" (20:9).

If we try to find in this scene a timetable for specific events leading to the end of history, we immediately run into difficulty. The nations had already been destroyed with the beast and the false prophet before the millennial period began (19:20–21). And John offers no explanation for their sudden reappearance. John is not writing a calendar for the end of the world; he is writing literature of encouragement to a people in the midst of crisis. He presents two scenarios, both of which assure Christians facing persecution under the Roman emperor Domitian that God is in control of human history and that God's justice will ultimately prevail. In his vision of the millennial period, John has pictured a this-worldly reign of God, which would fulfill the promise of traditional prophecy. Now he moves to the apocalyptic expectation of the end of this world and the final defeat of Satan.

Satan's final collapse happens so quickly, it seems anticlimactic: "And fire came down from heaven and consumed them. And the devil who had deceived them was thrown into the lake of fire and sulfur, where the beast and the false prophet were, and they will be tormented day and night forever and ever" (20:9–10). The victory over Satan involves no human action. In Revelation, the use of passive voice, "the devil . . . *was thrown* into the lake of fire," denotes God's action. Fire had often been associated with the manifestation of God ever since the time of the Exodus when God spoke to Moses from a burning bush and later appeared on Mount Sinai "like a devouring fire" (Exod. 3:2; 24:17). In the intertestamental literature and in the New Testament, destructive fire increasingly represented God's judgment (1 Enoch 18:11; Matt. 3:10; 5:22; 13:40; 25:41; Mark 9:43, 48; Luke 17:29; 2 Pet. 3:7). In Revelation, fire consumes not only God's human enemies, but also Satan, the instigator of all evil. Even death itself is thrown into the lake of fire (20:14).

Finally, John sees a great white throne and the One who sits on it. The dead, great and small, stand before the throne, and books are opened. The dead are judged "according to their works, as recorded in the books" (20:11–12). In the letters to seven churches in Revelation 1–3, the angel repeatedly warned the churches, "I know your works" (2:2, 19; 3:1, 8, 15). Now God judges all people according to their works. For John, faith and works cannot be separated.

All Things New

The scene changes radically in chapter 21. John beholds a new heaven and a new earth. "The first heaven and the first earth" have passed away. "The sea [is] no more" (21:1–3). In Revelation, Satan embodied the primordial sea dragon whom the gods of Near Eastern mythology had engaged in mortal combat at the creation of the earth. Various Old Testament texts referred to this monster as "River" or "Sea."[12] With Satan's death, no vestige of this watery chaos remains. John sees the holy city, the New Jerusalem, coming down from heaven and announces that God will now dwell among mortals, and that death, mourning, and pain will be no more (21:2–4). John hears the voice of the One seated on the throne, saying, "See, I am making all things new" (21:5).

Describing the New Jerusalem, John proclaims "the nations will walk by its light, and the kings of the earth will bring their glory into it" (21:24). This comes as a surprise because in Revelation 19:19–21, the "kings of the earth," all those who were deceived by Satan and did not worship the God of Israel, had been cast into the fiery lake of judgment. In contrast, this scene seems to suggest that God and the Lamb will make *all* things new, even "the nations" that had worshiped Satan and God's enemies who had already been judged according to their works. These two contradictory views, salvation for all versus salvation for faithful Christians only, stand side by side in Revelation. And again we note that John is not writing an analytical statement of doctrine or a calendar for the end of time. His pictorial language emphasizes human responsibility, asserting that God's justice will ultimately prevail. At the same time, it portrays a God who truly wishes to redeem the entire creation.

Interpretations for Christians Today

We have tried to understand what John's Apocalypse had to say to its original readers about the forces of evil, which must have seemed all-powerful to Christians who faced persecution for their beliefs. Now we are ready to consider its enduring message for people of faith who are living near the dawn of the twenty-first century.

The conflict between good and evil is a struggle in every generation. While most Christians today do not face the threat of exile or death for their beliefs, the way of Jesus Christ is still at odds with many of the prevailing values of our society. The twin commandments to love God and love neighbor are as difficult today as they have ever been—and as costly. Students of modern history have no trouble identifying rulers such as Revelation's "beast" who misuse their authority for the sake of personal gain. And we have our own "false prophets," some of whom champion their false gods from TV screens in our living rooms as they promote the worship of youth, sex, success, beauty, and pleasure.

In a nation where isms such as materialism, racism, classism, and militarism wield mighty power, we may wonder if these forces will destroy us. In a culture that values individuality over the welfare of the whole, wealth over honesty, power over compassion, popularity over virtue, status over integrity, and instant gratification over concern for future generations, we may ask, "Can Christ's way possibly triumph? Is evil too powerful to resist? Is there any hope for the way of self-sacrificing love? Is God still with us? Can God help us?"

To these questions, the answers of John's Apocalypse come to us from across the centuries. Love is stronger than hate. Good is stronger than evil. God is more powerful than Satan. God is with us. In the end, God will triumph. And God has the power to make all things new.

While John proclaimed "the time is near" (1:3), and "I [Christ] am coming soon" (22:12), Revelation did not counsel Christians to worry about the date when Christ would return to usher in the new age. In the message John brought from Christ to the church of Sardis, Christ said, "I will come like a thief, and you will not know at what hour I will come to you" (3:3).

The end-time events did not come "soon" in any ordinary understanding of the word "soon." Yet we can identify with John's sense of urgency. For each of us, our time on earth is brief. And we will pass this way but once. Although we are not to squander our energies trying to unlock the secrets of the future or to probe mysteries that are beyond the human province, the time to turn away from evil and to turn toward God is *now*.

For the time that remains to each of us—and only God knows how much time that is—Revelation's message is clear. *Live your faith!* Revelation urges us to commit ourselves to Christ and to Christ's purposes with confidence and joy, celebrating in advance God's certain victory. In one of the few sentences where God speaks directly to John, God says, "I am the Alpha and the Omega" (21:6). A few verses later, Christ the Lamb pronounces the same words, for there is no separation between God and Christ in Revelation. "I am the Alpha and the

Omega," proclaims Christ, the first and the last, the beginning and the end (22:13).

That is all we really need to know about the future. Ultimately, the end is God. Whenever and however the end comes, the God who is made known to us in Christ the Lamb will welcome us.

To Think About

1. Revelation 5 transforms the image of the Messiah as the "Lion of the tribe of Judah" into an image of a sacrificial lamb. Is your concept of God's Messiah more like a lion or a lamb? Do you see the role of Christ's followers as more lionlike or lamblike?

2. How would you respond to someone who told you that he or she was not really concerned about a worldwide buildup of nuclear weapons because a cataclysmic battle is part of God's plan?

3. In Revelation, the Lamb defeated Satan, the beast, and the false prophet by using the weapon of God's Word. How are you proclaiming God's Word, both in what you say and in what you do? How is your congregation proclaiming God's Word?

4. Do you agree that John of Patmos is not writing a calendar for the end of history? What do you see as the dangers or benefits of attempting to predict the end of the world?

5. While John emphasizes faith, he also states that all persons will be judged by their works. How do you reconcile these two ideas? How would you define "faith"?

6. Although our faith today is not tested by a commandment to worship a foreign emperor, the way of Jesus Christ continues to be at odds with the prevailing values of our society. What messages does Revelation have for us as we confront evil in our society today?

7. Revelation asserts that Christ's power of self-sacrificing love is stronger than the power of evil (Satan). Do you believe that love is stronger than hate and that good is stronger than evil? Why or why not? How does your answer to this question make a difference in your actions?

CONCLUSION: SATAN AND PERSONAL FAITH

In the introduction to this book, I invited you to join me in a search for answers to some questions about Satan and the Bible that are important for Christians today. Can we take the Bible seriously and still ignore the figure of Satan, who clearly had a place in New Testament thought? What does the Bible really say about Satan? What do I believe about Satan? How can I talk about my belief? And how does this belief affect my life?

To the first question, Can we take the Bible seriously and still ignore the figure of Satan? I believe the answer is no. I admit that as a UCC minister, I glossed over the Bible's references to Satan for many years. But questions continued to arise. In almost every Bible study I led, participants raised issues about Satan. Popular movies dealt with the subject. The turn of the millennium provoked interest in Satan's role in end-time scenarios. My children asked me questions I could not answer. Finally, I began to wonder, What does the Bible really say about Satan?

My quest for an answer to this question has been the subject of the main body of this book. Here is a brief summary of the insights I have gained.

Satan in the Bible

There is no single answer to the question, What does the Bible say about Satan? The Bible was written during a period of some fourteen hundred years, and each of its books reflects the thinking of its own time. The Old Testament knew no supernatural ruler of evil. *Satan,* at first, was simply a common Hebrew noun meaning "adversary" or "opponent." In later parts of the Old Testament, Satan became more personalized. As a member of God's heavenly court, Satan acted as a prosecuting attorney, always with God's permission.

A supernatural ruler of evil first appeared in Judaism with the rise of apocalyptic literature during the four hundred years that elapsed between the end of the Old Testament and the beginning of the New Testament. The apocalyptic authors of First Enoch, Jubilees, and other intertestamental books addressed the concerns of orthodox Jews who watched helplessly while their Jewish brothers and sisters adopted the ideas and lifestyle of their Greek conquerors. These apocalyptic books answered their questions about God's goodness, power, and faithfulness. The world's injustice was not God's doing; evil had been instigated by a supernatural enemy with whom God was engaged in cosmic combat. But God's victory was certain, and faithfulness would be rewarded. The apocalyptic writers looked with hope and confidence toward the consummation of earthly history when God would usher in a new age and reign forever in justice and in peace.

By the time of Jesus, apocalypticism was a well-known strain of thought within Judaism, and belief in a supernatural ruler of evil was common. We cannot be sure whether Jesus understood Satan literally or whether he used "Satan" as a metaphor for the power of evil. A quick review of the four references to Satan that are common to more than one Synoptic Gospel illustrates the problem. (1) The account of Jesus' temptation in the wilderness had no witnesses; thus, the details of the underlying historical incident are uncertain (Matt. 4:1–11; Mark 1:12–13; Luke 4:1–13).[1] (2) The reference to Satan in the interpretation of the parable of the sower appears to be a later addition to Jesus' original parable (Matt. 13:18–23; Mark 4:13–20; Luke 8:11–15).[2] (3) When Jesus asked the Pharisees, "How can Satan cast out Satan?" he might have echoed his accusers' terms in order to refute them as he answered critics who accused him of healing by the power of the Prince of Demons (Mark 3:23; see also Matt. 12:26; Luke 11:18).[3] (4) When Jesus rebuked Peter, saying, "Get behind me, Satan," he might have used "Satan" as a metaphor for powerful temptation, much as we might say, "Don't tempt me, you devil!" (Matt. 16:13–23; Mark 8:27–33; Luke 9:18–22).[4] Jesus did not necessarily imply that a supernatural power dwelt in Peter. Not one of the four references to Satan that are common to the Synoptic Gospels provides strong evidence that Jesus conceived of Satan as a literal being.

For the apostle Paul, a ruler of evil was clearly literal. However, as we saw in chapter 7, Paul's writing contains surprisingly few references to Satan, and in these references, the apostle portrayed Satan in a variety of roles, ranging from teacher to the god of this world. In later New Testament books, including Revelation, Satan is a literal figure. Yet even Revelation's Satan has a mythic dimension, for it embodies the primordial dragon of Near Eastern mythology.

Taking Satan Seriously

What, then, do I believe about Satan?

Looking at the variety of interpretations of the figure of Satan that are found in the Bible, I find it difficult to conceive of Satan as a literal being. But that does not mean that I dismiss the biblical Satan as irrelevant. Quite the contrary, I take the Bible's Satan language very seriously.

Evil is all too real in our world today. And it is certainly larger than personal sin. Evil has collective and cumulative power. Cultures of poverty and drugs, for example, flourish amidst group pressures whose destructive influence is passed from generation to generation. Racism and sexism are the results of habits of injustice, perpetuated across the centuries. Families and individuals sometimes struggle against forces they experience as demonic. Personal temptation can be so overwhelming, it seems to take on a personality of its own. For evil so large, "Satan" is an appropriate metaphor.

How do I talk about Satan in a culture that tends either to believe in a literal and supernatural ruler of evil or to dismiss the whole idea as irrelevant nonsense? With my children and grandchildren, I try to be clear about what I believe. I say, "I think that 'Satan' is one of the Bible's ways of talking about bad things in the world and about feelings inside us that make us want to do things that are wrong." As they grow up, children will hear many different ideas about Satan, and eventually, they will come to their own conclusions. But they want and need to know what their parents believe.

With adults, I am equally honest, but I try to avoid arguing about the question of whether or not Satan is real. My reluctance to debate this issue stems in part from my desire to respect the right of others to hold opinions that are different from mine. But it is more than that. I do not believe that the question of whether "Satan" is literal or metaphoric language is the central issue for those of us who sincerely want to understand the Bible's Satan language and apply it to our lives. The central issue is what the Bible's Satan language teaches us about the power of evil and the way we are to respond to it. Usually when the name of Satan comes up in a discussion, the issue is not whether or not Satan is literal; the discussion is about something else. Another issue lies behind the Satan language. If we listen closely, we will hear underlying messages such as these:

"I strongly disagree with you."

"I think a certain kind of behavior is wrong."

"I feel threatened by this idea."

"You are an evil person."

"Be a good girl!"

"I'm very concerned about things I see happening in our town (church/nation/world)."

· "Life just isn't fair."

"I'm struggling with an overwhelming temptation."

"I really couldn't help what I did."

"I feel helpless in the face of the problems in my life, my community, or the world."

The Bible's Satan language, whether understood literally or figuratively, speaks to real issues in my life and yours. It speaks to issues of power, weakness, responsibility, justice, sin and its consequences, judgment, forgiveness, compassion, fear, love, and hope. Even the Satan cults that attract some young people today are rarely about the worship of a supernatural power. Underneath the Satan language, these cults are about power and powerlessness, rejection, anger, despair, and rebellion against the religion of their parents and other authority figures.[5] I believe that the most helpful way Christians can talk with one another about Satan is by focusing on the underlying issues that the Satan language is addressing. We might say, "You really disagree with _____ about _____," or "I hear you saying you feel helpless in this situation," or "I don't like to label anyone as an instrument of Satan; I think that kind of judgment belongs to God."

Taking the Bible's Satan language seriously means interpreting its message about the issues it is addressing in ways that are faithful to the biblical text. The Bible's Satan language has been interpreted and misinterpreted throughout the last twenty centuries. Whether we are reading the Bible, listening to the explanations of others including preachers, discussing our views with friends, or answering the questions of our children, we need criteria to help us decide whether a particular interpretation is valid. A valid interpretation may take Satan literally or metaphorically. But it will not distort the message of the biblical text about the evil in our lives and the way we are to respond to it.

Criteria for Interpreting the Bible's Satan Language

Based on the Bible's treatment of the figure of Satan, here are some criteria for valid interpretation of the Bible's Satan language:

- Does it emphasize personal responsibility?
- Does it urge us to resist evil without demonizing our opponents?
- Does it calm our fears?
- Does it call us to active faith?
- Does it move us to faithful action in the here and now?
- Does it proclaim the gospel?

Does the interpretation emphasize personal responsibility? The Bible's Satan language is often interpreted in ways that suggest that human beings are helpless victims of a supernatural power. Yet the apostle Paul asserted that those who are "in Christ" are freed from bondage to sin and evil, which he occasionally represented as "Satan" but more often called "the flesh." Jesus resisted temptation in the wilderness by remembering the law of Moses.

Revelation emphasized that human beings choose whether to follow Satan or to follow Christ and that all will stand in judgment before God. These texts do not indicate that "Satan" is an adequate excuse for human failings.

Does the interpretation urge us to resist evil without demonizing our opponents? The Bible is sometimes interpreted in ways that label other people as instruments of Satan. Yet we see the danger of taking the authority for such judgment upon ourselves in the incident where Pharisees accused Jesus of healing with Satan's power (Matt. 12:25–37; Mark 3:23–30; Luke 11:17–23). The temptation to demonize our opponents is very human. It is easier to judge than it is to step in and help. And it is easier to see the work of "Satan" in others than to acknowledge it in ourselves. That is probably why Jesus cautioned, "Do not judge, so that you may not be judged" (Matt. 7:1; Luke 6:37).

Even in Revelation, which placed heavy emphasis on judgment, we find no suggestion that judgment belongs to anyone but God and Christ. While John expected God to judge Christ's opponents severely, he made it plain that the only ways Christians were to deal with their enemies were to proclaim the Word and to follow in the way of Christ the Lamb.

The Bible's Satan language names evil as real and powerful. And it calls us to resist persons, ideas, and political movements we believe are wrong. But to label another person or group as "of Satan" moves into the realm of ultimate judgment. And ultimate judgment belongs to God!

Does the interpretation calm our fears? My granddaughter returns home from playing with a friend and tells her mother, "Satan comes up out of the ground like a fiery hand to grab you!" The Bible's Satan language has been interpreted in ways that foster a religion that uses fear and the threat of punishment as its primary motivation. A religion based on fear is not healthy for children or for adults. Not only does it breed nightmares and foster insecurity, it misrepresents the teaching of the One who summed up all the law in the twin commandments to love God and love neighbor. A fear-based religion becomes a religion of "don'ts." Obedience springs not from love of God, but from fear of God's wrath. Even acts of "kindness" arise out of the need to earn God's favor rather than out of genuine love for God's family.

A fear-based religion usually draws heavily on Revelation to support its doctrine of reward and punishment. While neither Revelation nor any other book of the Bible contains an image of a fiery hand that emerges from the ground, Revelation does contain equally bizarre and frightening images of God's judgment. A beast that rears up from a bottomless pit to conquer and kill, great birds that devour the flesh of those who follow the beast, and especially the eternal punishment in a lake of fire that awaits anyone whose name is not written in the book of life—these are terrifying pictures (Rev. 11:7; 19:21; 20:14–15). We cannot explain away these images of judgment. They convey clear warnings about the consequences of sin and faithlessness. Although we take these warnings seriously, we should also remember that they were not intended to inspire fear. Quite the opposite! Revelation was literature of *reassurance* to Christians in crisis. Revelation was not a warning to those who stood outside the Christian faith; it was a word of encouragement to church members in desperate circumstances.

The message of Revelation, and of all the Bible's apocalyptic literature, is that faithful followers of Christ have nothing to fear. God controls human destiny, and in God's time and way, justice will prevail. The future is in the hands of the God who loves us, forgives us, and grants us new beginnings. Even in death, we are safe in God's hands.

Does the interpretation call us to active faith? My granddaughter tells her mother, "When Satan comes up out of the ground to grab you, just say, 'Jesus, Jesus,' and Satan will go away." Adult Christians, too, may use the words, "I believe in Jesus," as a kind of magic formula that will overcome "Satan" and guarantee right relationship with God. This interpretation of the Bible's Satan language can create the impression that saying the right words or giving intellectual assent to the right doctrines is what Christian faith is all about.

Salvation by faith is a core Christian belief, one that I accept wholeheartedly. But faith is more than words. It is more than believing the right things. This is the issue Jesus addressed when he rebuked Peter at Caesarea Philippi for trying to talk Jesus out of the journey to the cross. Peter had already confessed Jesus as the Christ. He had said the right words. But he was not ready to commit his life to following the way of the Christ. "Get behind me, Satan!" Jesus said to Peter (Matt. 16:23; Mark 8:33). To separate belief from action is wrong, even demonic.

The apostle Paul also called Christians to live their faith, telling them that a life lived "in Christ" would produce "fruit" of the Spirit: "love, joy, peace, patience, kindness, generosity, faithfulness, gentleness, and self-control" (Gal. 5:22–23). Life in Christ would look radically different from a life Paul described as enslaved to the "flesh," to "sin," and occasionally to the power of "Satan."

Like Jesus and Paul, John of Patmos stressed the connection between faith and action. To the seven churches of Asia, the Christ of Revelation said repeatedly, "I know your works" (Rev. 2:2, 19; 3:1, 8, 15). True faith is active faith.

Does the interpretation move us to faithful action in the here and now? The Bible's Satan language has been used to project a timetable for the end of human history, the coming of a new heaven and a new earth. Yet undue emphasis on end-time events can lead to the neglect of care for this world in the here and now. We may say, "Since the end is coming soon and Christ will win the battle against evil, we have nothing to do but wait." Predictions of end-time events usually draw heavily on Revelation. However in Revelation, Christ warned of the futility of this kind of speculation: "I will come like a thief, and you will not know at what hour I will come to you" (3:3).

In the only apocalyptic sermon Jesus preached, according to the Synoptic Gospels, Jesus warned against looking for signs of the coming of the end (Matt. 24; Mark 13; Luke 21). "About that day or hour no one knows, neither the angels in heaven, nor the Son, but only the Father. Beware, keep alert; for you do not know when the time will come" (Mark 13:32–33). In a parable, Jesus compared the role of his faithful followers to slaves whom a master left in charge of his property while he went away on a journey. "Blessed is that slave whom his master will find *at work,*" Jesus said (Matt. 24:45–46, emphasis added; see also Mark 13:34–37). We are stewards of God's earth. To predict the time of the Master's return is not our job. Our mission is to live faithfully day by day, so that however and whenever the hour arrives, the returning Master will find us *at work.*

Does the interpretation proclaim the gospel? In Revelation, God and Christ overcame Satan and Satan's followers with the "weapon" of God's Word (Rev. 1:16; 2:16; 19:15, 21). In the parable of the sower, Jesus urged his followers to heed God's Word, the seed sown along the path, so that Satan could not steal it away (Matt. 13:18–19; Mark 4:14–15; Luke 8:11–12). In both cases, the Word refers to the gospel message, the good news! It is the good news that God loves us and desires our love in return. It is the good news that God in Christ loved us enough to die for us. It is the good news that through Christ's act of self-sacrificing love, we are brought into right relationship with God. The entire New Testament urges every reader and listener to trust God's good news and to live in thankful response. We are to follow God's commandments, not because we want to avoid punishment, but because they are written on our hearts. We are to reach out to our neighbor in love, not because we feel compelled out of a sense of duty, but because God first loved us. We are to deal with enemies, not by returning evil for evil, but by trusting the power of self-sacrificing love. Any reading of scripture that distorts or negates the gospel message steals the "seed," the Word that the sower has spread over the ground.

Yes, the Bible's Satan language reminds us that evil is real and powerful in our world, and that it is larger than personal sin. "Satan" is not too strong a metaphor to represent evil's more-than-personal power. But the message of the Bible's Satan language is clear. God is more powerful than Satan; good is stronger than evil; love is stronger than hate.

The Bible's Satan language, rightly interpreted, is thoroughly consistent with the message proclaimed throughout the whole of scripture. Love and serve God with your whole heart. Follow Christ in the way of self-sacrificing love. Bear the fruit of the Spirit. Put aside fear. Trust God's power. Accept God's grace. Praise and thank God day by day. Live in hope. And celebrate! In the present and in the future, you belong to God.

To Think About

1. How have your ideas about the biblical Satan changed through reading this book?

2. What insights have been most helpful? What have been troubling?

3. What would you teach your children, grandchildren, or other children in your life about Satan?

4. How would you answer someone who asked you, "Do you believe in Satan?"

5. What messages do you now see in the Bible's Satan language about the following issues:

- Personal responsibility?
- Judgment and compassion?
- God's Word?
- Human weakness and divine power?
- Faith?
- Self-sacrificing love?

NOTES

Introduction

1. John Hagee, *Beginning of the End* (Nashville: Thomas Nelson, 1996); Ed Hindson, *Approaching Armageddon* (Eugene, Oreg.: Harvest House, 1997); David Jeremiah, *Escape the Coming Night* (Dallas: Word, 1990).

1. Satan in the Old Testament

1. Some other possible translations are "the Lord our God, the Lord is one," or "the Lord our God is one Lord."

2. Here and throughout this book, when I note "references to Satan," I am speaking of the Hebrew or Greek manuscripts. English translations vary, and some may use the word "Satan" where it does not appear in the original language.

3. For a more complete discussion of the conflict, see Elaine Pagels, *The Origin of Satan* (New York: Vintage Books, division of Random House, 1995), 43–44.

4. Ibid., 42.

5. Walter Brueggemann, *Genesis: Interpretation Bible Commentary* (Atlanta: John Knox Press, 1982), 47.

6. *Zaphon* is Hebrew for "the north." The Revised Standard Version translates this line "I will sit on the mount of assembly in the far north."

7. Ugartic (Ras Shamra) Text 49:I:35–37, translated by Cyrus H. Gordon, *Ugaritic Literature: A Comprehensive Translation of the Poetic and Prose Texts* (Rome: Pontificiom Institutum Biblicum, 1949), 44. Also see M. Eugene Boring, *Revelation: Interpretation Bible Commentary* (Louisville: John Knox Press, 1989), 137.

8. Ugartic (Ras Shamra) Text 'nt:III:36–39, in Gordon, *Ugaritic Literature,* 50. Note the similarity between this passage and Isaiah 27:1.

9. *Enuma Elis,* Tablet IV:33–146, translated by Alexander Heidel, *The Babylonian Genesis* (Chicago: University of Chicago Press, 1942), 28–32.

2. Satan between the Testaments

1. Daniel is apparently "Danel" mentioned in Ezekiel 14:14; 28:3. Danel was associated with patriarchs of Canaanite myth. The dating of Daniel is debated by some scholars; however, a large majority of scholars and a preponderant weight of evidence support a date around 165 B.C.E. For a good discussion of the evidence for this date, see George W. Anderson, *A Critical Introduction to the Old Testament* (London: Duckworth, 1974), 209–15, and Bernard W. Anderson, *Understanding the Old Testament,* 3rd ed. (Englewood Cliffs, N.J.: Prentice Hall, 1975), 576–77.

2. The Writings, a collection of works that circulated independently, were not gathered into final form within the Hebrew canon until after Rome destroyed Jerusalem in 70 C.E. A Jewish Council at Jamnia in the year 90 closed the canon.

3. The best-known collection is R. H. Charles, *The Apocrypha and Pseudepigrapha in the Old Testament* (Oxford: Oxford University Press, 1963).

4. Translated by Charles, *Apocrypha and Pseudepigrapha.* All subsequent quotations from First Enoch are taken from Charles's translation. The story in First Enoch is an expansion of a brief account in Genesis 6 in which the sons of God took human wives and bore giants called Nephilim.

5. Elements of early apocalyptic thought are also found in some postexilic writings in the Old Testament, especially Isaiah 24–27; 56–66; Ezekiel 38–39; 40–48. The book of Daniel is the only complete apocalypse in the Old Testament.

6. Charles states that "Enoch vi–xvi, xxiii–xxxvi were known to the *Book of Jubilees,*" and that in places the author "reproduces his source so faithfully that he leaves the persons unchanged, and forgets to adapt this fragment to its new context" (*Apocrypha and Pseudepigrapha,* 7). Charles dates Jubilees at 153–105 B.C.E., after Judas Maccabeus drove out Antiochus Epiphanes. George W. Nickelsburg, *Jewish Literature Between the Bible and the Mishnah* (Philadelphia: Fortress Press, 1981), 77, believes the date of Jubilees can be no later than 176 B.C.E. since there is no specific reference to Antiochus Epiphanes.

7. Some other apocalyptic works where a supernatural ruler of evil appears are Second Enoch, Sibylline Oracles Three & Four, Testaments of the Twelve Patriarchs, and Life of Adam and Eve.

8. War Rule (1QM) 1:1. The text of the War Rule can be found in Geza Vermes, *The Dead Sea Scrolls in English,* 3rd ed. (London: Penguin Books, 1987), 123–45.

9. John R. Himmels, *Persian Mythology* (London: Hamlyn Publishing Group, 1973), 13–15.

10. "Epiphanes," meaning "God made manifest," was the presumptuous title added to his name by Antiochus IV.

11. For a concise summary of the rise of Hellenism in Judea see Robert C. Dentan, *The Apocrypha: Bridge of the Testaments* (Greenwich: Seabury Press, 1954), 41.

12. In Daniel, evil angels, when they are mentioned, represent the patron saints of Israel's enemies. See Daniel 10:12–14.

13. Pagels, *Origin of Satan,* 50–51. Pagels credits George W. E. Nickelsburg, "Apocalyptic and Myth in 1 *Enoch* 6–11," *Journal of Biblical Literature* 96 (1977): 383–405.

14. Ibid., 49, emphasis in original.

3. Satan and Personal Responsibility

1. Of the four Gospels, Luke contains the most references to Satan. Many of these references seem to be editorial additions to material that in Matthew or Mark contained no reference to Satan. For example, only Luke and John state that Satan entered Judas (Luke 22:3; John 13:27). Only Luke's account has Jesus refer to Satan at the Last Supper when he says Peter will deny him three times (Luke 22:31–34; Matt. 26:33–35; Mark 14:29–31; John 13:31–38).

2. Jim Wallis, *A Call to Conversion* (San Francisco: Harper & Row, 1981), 49.

4. Satan and Compassion

1. In *The Five Gospels: What Did Jesus Really Say?,* translation and commentary by Robert W. Funk, Roy W. Hoover, and the Jesus Seminar (New York: Scribner, Polebridge Press, 1993), Luke 11:17–22 is printed in pink (329–30), signifying that Jesus "probably said something like this" (36).

2. In Luke, the man was simply unable to speak. In Matthew, he was also blind. Mark does not introduce the story with a specific healing, but has the scribes, who have heard about Jesus' healing, come down from Jerusalem. Jesus' response, however, clearly indicates that Jesus' healings are the background of Mark's story as well.

3. In Matthew, Jesus' critics were Pharisees; in Mark, they were scribes; in Luke, they were simply "some of them."

4. Although translated "Beelzebub" in the Latin Vulgate and the King James Version, almost all Greek manuscripts use "Beelzebul." The name probably derives from the Canaanite god Baalzebul, meaning "supreme god" or "god of the temple." Baalzebub in 2 Kings 1:2 was a contemptuous corruption of Baalzebul. Baalzebub means "Lord of flies."

5. Satan and Self-Sacrificing Love

1. For a comprehensive discussion of the significance of this decision, see my book *Journey to the Cross* (Cleveland, Ohio: United Church Press, 1996), 1–11.

2. Luke's version contains no mention of Satan.

3. Literally translated, the line reads, "For you are not on the side of God, but of men."

4. Luke places the same story in the context of the Last Supper (22:24–27).

6. Satan and the Word

1. C. H. Dodd, *The Parables of the Kingdom* (New York: Charles Scribner's Sons, 1961), 3.

2. John Dominic Crossan, *In Parables* (New York: Harper & Row, 1973), 51.

3. Matthew says "the evil one"; Mark says "Satan"; Luke says "the devil."

7. Satan and the Spiritual Life

1. The New Revised Standard Version ascribes the thirteen letters listed to Paul. The King James Version ascribes Hebrews in addition, but Hebrews is almost universally acknowledged to be a work of a different author. See Reginald H. Fuller, *A Critical Introduction to the New Testament* (London: Duckworth, 1979), 5.

2. Ibid.

3. Rom. 16:20, 1 Thess. 2:9, 3:3 (the evil one), 1 Cor. 5:5, 7:5, 10:10 (the destroyer), 2 Cor. 2:11, 4:4 (god of this world), 6:15 (Beliar), 11:14, and 12:7.

4. For an excellent discussion on this point see Robin Scroggs, *Paul for a New Day* (Philadelphia: Fortress Press, 1977), 9.

5. George Arthur Buttrick, ed., *The Interpreter's Dictionary of the Bible*, vol. 1 (Nashville: Abingdon, 1996), 73.

6. Some special Lukan material (material not found in either Matthew or Mark) holds a similar understanding of Satan's role in the world. For example, in describing the kingdoms of the world in the story of Jesus' temptation in the wilderness, Satan says, "To you I will give their glory and all this authority; *for it has been given over to me, and I give it to anyone I please*" (Luke 4:6, emphasis added). See also Luke 10:18.

8. Satan and Hope

1. Boring, *Revelation: Interpretation*, 48.

2. Other dates have been argued, but this dating seems the most likely. See Fuller, *Introduction to the New Testament*, 187–88; Boring, *Revelation: Interpre-*

tation, 9–10; Bruce M. Metzger and Roland E. Murphy, eds., *The New Oxford Annotated Bible* (New York: Oxford University Press, 1991), 364; Martin Rist, "The Revelation of St. John the Divine," in *The Interpreter's Bible*, vol. 12 (New York: Abingdon, 1957), 356.

3. See Fuller, *Introduction to the New Testament*, 186, for a brief summary of the evidence against John of Patmos as the author of the Fourth Gospel.

4. Boring, *Revelation: Interpretation*, 12.

5. Rist, *Interpreter's Bible*, 12:356.

6. For a listing of some of the other apocalyptic works they might have known, see note 7 in chapter 2 of this book.

7. Boring, *Revelation: Interpretation*, 150.

8. For a more detailed discussion of this heavenly drama, see Boring, *Revelation: Interpretation*, 150–63.

9. Ugaritic (Ras Shamra) Text 'nt:III:36–39, in Gordon, *Ugaritic Literature*, 50. See chapter 1 of this book and note 8 to chapter 1.

10. "Day Star" is translated "Lucifer" in the King James Version. See the discussion of Lucifer in chapter 1 of this book.

11. See chapter 2 for a fuller discussion.

12. I am following Dr. Boring's interpretation (*Revelation: Interpretation*, 158). Rist interprets this line to mean that Jesus was "taken from one place in heaven to the presence of God, and was there enthroned" (*Interpreter's Bible*, 12:455).

13. Genesis 6:1–4 formed the biblical text from which the stories of watcher angels were later constructed.

14. Rist, *Interpreter's Bible*, 12:461; Boring, *Revelation: Interpretation*, 155–56.

15. See the note on 2 Esdras 12:11 in the *New Oxford Annotated Bible*, 330 AP.

16. Boring, *Revelation: Interpretation*, 163; Rist, *Interpreter's Bible*, 12:466; *New Oxford Annotated Bible*, 378.

17. For example, Revelation 5:13 portrays all creatures in heaven, on earth, and under the earth united in singing praise to the Lamb. Revelation 15:4 states, "All nations will come and worship before you." And in the description of the New Jerusalem, John states, "The nations will walk by its light, and the kings of the earth will bring their glory into it" (Rev. 21:24). Since "the nations" in John means *pagan* nations, this suggests that ultimate salvation is universal.

9. Satan and the Armies of Heaven

1. *New Oxford Annotated Bible*, note on Revelation 16:16, 380 NT. Compare Judges 5:19; 2 Kings 9:27; 2 Chronicles 35:22. "Armageddon" has a variety of spellings in the Greek manuscripts and is rendered "Harmagedon" in the New Revised Standard Version.

2. The beast is represented in 17:1 as "many waters."

3. See also 2 Esdras 12:31–32, written about the same time as Revelation.

4. Jim Durlesser's essay "The Lion Is a Lamb," in *Approaching the New Millennium,* ed. Eleanor A. Moore (Nashville: Cokesbury, 1995), 56–61, is an insightful discussion of the transformation of the image of the Lion of the tribe of Judah into a sacrificial lamb.

5. Rist notes the parallels between the Jews' miraculous deliverance from their Egyptian oppressors after a series of devastating plagues and the liberation of Christians from their Roman persecutors after a series of similar woes (*Interpreter's Bible,* 12:407). The woes and plagues in Revelation have many parallels in the Exodus story.

6. In Isaiah 63:1–3, the source of John's imagery in this passage, a mighty conqueror emerges from battle in garments stained with the blood of Israel's enemies. John transforms the imagery.

7. See the discussion under "Supernatural Ruler of Evil" in chapter 2 of this book.

8. See also the discussion of watcher angels in chapter 2 of this book.

9. Boring, *Revelation: Interpretation,* 206–7.

10. *New Oxford Annotated Bible,* note on Ezekiel 38:1–39:29, 1108–9 OT.

11. In the apocalyptic tradition of John's time, Ezekiel's "Gog of Magog" had become "Gog and Magog." Rist notes, "In some sources, Gog and Magog would make their appearance [for the ultimate battle] before the messianic reign; in others, during it; and in still others, as in Revelation, following the kingdom of the Messiah" (*Interpreter's Bible,* 12:522).

12. See chapter 1 of this book.

Conclusion

1. See chapter 3 of this book.

2. See chapter 6 of this book.

3. See chapter 4 of this book.

4. See chapter 5 of this book.

5. An excellent book on this subject is Joyce Mercer, *Behind the Mask of Adolescent Satanism* (Minneapolis: Deaconess Press, 1991).

SELECTED BIBLIOGRAPHY

Anderson, Bernard W. *Understanding the Old Testament.* 3rd ed. Englewood Cliffs, N.J.: Prentice Hall, 1975.

Anderson, George W. *A Critical Introduction to the Old Testament.* London: Duckworth, 1974.

Boring, M. Eugene. *Revelation: Interpretation Bible Commentary.* Louisville: John Knox Press, 1989.

Brueggemann, Walter. *Genesis: Interpretation Bible Commentary.* Atlanta: John Knox Press, 1982.

Charles, R. H. *The Apocrypha and Pseudepigrapha in the Old Testament.* Oxford: Oxford University Press, 1963.

Crossan, John Dominic. *In Parables.* New York: Harper & Row, 1973.

Dentan, Robert C. *The Apocrypha, Bridge of the Testaments.* Greenwich: Seabury Press, 1954.

Dodd, C. H. *The Parables of the Kingdom.* New York: Charles Scribner's Sons, 1961.

Fuller, Reginald H. *A Critical Introduction to the New Testament.* London: Duckworth, 1979.

Funk, Robert W., Roy W. Hoover, and the Jesus Seminar, eds. *The Five Gospels: What Did Jesus Really Say?* New York: Scribner, Polebridge Press, 1993.

Gordon, Cyrus H. *Ugaritic Literature: A Comprehensive Translation of the Poetic and Prose Texts.* Rome: Pontificiom Institutum Biblicum, 1949.

Heidel, Alexander. *The Babylonian Genesis.* Chicago: University of Chicago Press, 1942.

Himmels, John R. *Persian Mythology.* London: Hamlyn Publishing Group, 1973.

Metzger, Bruce M., and Roland E. Murphy, eds. *The New Oxford Annotated Bible.* New York: Oxford University Press, 1991.

Moore, Eleanor A., ed. *Approaching the New Millennium.* Nashville: Cokesbury, 1995.

Nagel, Myra B. *Journey to the Cross.* Cleveland, Ohio: United Church Press, 1996.

Nickelsburg, George W. *Jewish Literature Between the Bible and the Mishnah.* Philadelphia: Fortress Press, 1981.

Pagels, Elaine. *The Origin of Satan.* New York: Vintage Books, division of Random House, 1995.

Rist, Martin. "The Revelation of St. John the Divine." In *The Interpreter's Bible.* Vol. 12. New York: Abingdon, 1957.

Scroggs, Robin. *Paul for a New Day.* Philadelphia: Fortress Press, 1977.

Vermes, Geza. *The Dead Sea Scrolls in English.* 3rd ed. London: Penguin Books, 1987.

Wallis, Jim. *A Call to Conversion.* San Francisco: Harper & Row, 1981.